Mud on My Knees

Cultivating the Soil of Your Prodigal's Heart

Prayer Guide and Journal

Debra Bosacki

For they are transplanted

into the Lord's own garden and

are under His personal care.

Psalm 92:13 (TLB)

Published by Garden of the Heart Ministries

Mud on My Knees

Garden of the Heart Prayer Guide and Journal

In dedication to My Mother and Father,
the late Marie and Stephen Prenger,
whose lives inspired me and
taught me what it means to love <u>Unconditionally</u>!

I will give them a heart to know me, that I am the LORD. They will be my people, and I will be their God, for they will return to me with all their heart.
Jeremiah 24:7

Notes. . .

A Personal Word...

from Debra

*. . . O*n your knees and pray for harvest hands! Matthew 9:38 (MSG)

Mud on my knees! Why am I here? My knees hurt ... my back hurts ... spring flowers are only a dream. All I see is dirt, disgusting worm-infested dirt. What good can come of THIS? Why am I here? Why am I kneeling and praying in muddy soil?

There is nothing more frustrating than watching your loved ones drift away from God. When I was in the depths of that despair, I wondered, "Why can't they understand the truth when I share it with them?" No matter how much I tried, their hearts remained hardened.

But then ... but then, the Master Gardener revealed something that changed my life and I believe – no, I KNOW – it will change yours as well, if you join me in getting mud on your knees. Let's cultivate the ground of our wayward loved ones' hearts together through prayer. The Master Gardener is calling us to co-labor with Him in His garden, the Garden of the Heart. Listen to what He says:

> Everyone is going to end up kneeling before me.
> Everyone is going to end up saying of me, 'Yes!
> Salvation and strength are in God!'
> Isaiah 45:18 (MSG)

If you don't have a green thumb, take heart. I wasn't a gardener when God first gave me this word picture, and I can't say that I have a green thumb even now; but I have become a gardener in God's garden and you can as well, whether or not you till earthly soil.

Have you ever noticed that the Bible is filled with garden terminology revealing

13

God as the Master Gardener, cultivating the heart of man? This garden depicts a secret place of the heart, created to be filled with the beauty and life-giving presence of our Savior, Jesus Christ. I am so excited to show you how to cultivate the heart, pull down strongholds that are keeping your loved ones from God and plant seeds of prayer. As you labor together with the Holy Spirit, He will water and bring forth life until your loved ones' hearts are like a garden in full bloom, showcasing the love of Christ as their own faith is deepened and strengthened.

It is not just a time of praying for others though; you will grow as well as you seek Him with all of your heart. Do you long to be that close to Christ? Then read on. Within these pages are ways to cultivate and bring your garden to full bloom and harvest. You'll learn to see with God's eyes the things that we cannot see, when life's circumstances begin to overwhelm us and those we love. If you'll just stick with it and allow God to teach you as He so patiently taught me, your prayer garden WILL thrive, glowing in the light of Christ. Darkness cannot survive when Son-light shines on it.

> The light shines through the darkness, and the darkness can never extinguish it.
> John 1:5 (NLT)

You can cultivate hearts through prayer; both those who have fallen far from God, and those whom you sense have hearts starting to grow cold towards God. Or, use this journal proactively to protect your heart or the hearts of your loved ones. You can even use these concepts to avidly intercede for the lost, those who've never known Christ as Lord and Savior. Truly, it is a resource to help you help your loved ones live the abundant life they are destined to have in Christ.

Throughout this book I will use the term "prodigal" in reference to those whose hearts have strayed from God, although the concepts can be appropriately applied to any of us. A prodigal is someone who at one time received Christ as Lord and Savior, but has since shifted away from God and is no longer living in obedience to Him. Your wayward loved one might be a spouse, child, parent, brother, sister, friend, stranger or, possibly, you. At times, many of us have walked the prodigal path in one form or another.

The term "prodigal" comes from Jesus' parable in Luke 15:11-31. These verses depict the wayward loved one who fell deep into sin and lost close fellowship with his Father.

The major theme of this parable is the restoration of a believer into fellowship with his father. And it is a story of a father who is eagerly awaiting his son's return. The son had to learn the hard way that choosing this lifestyle would lead to heartache, dissatisfaction and disappointment.

Even though your lost loved one may have to go through some difficult lessons, there is hope! God will instruct you about how to cultivate his or her heart and plant the seed of His Word. Of prime importance, you'll learn how to cultivate your heart; for unless its soil is soft to the Master's touch, you won't be receptive to His instructions about how to pray for others. Remember, prayer is <u>relationship</u> not <u>performance</u>. Even when you don't know how to pray, the Holy Spirit will pray through you.

> In the same way, the Spirit helps us in our weakness. We do not know what we ought to pray for, but the Spirit himself intercedes for us with groans that words cannot express.
> Romans 8:26

As you use this prayer journal, expect to hear from your heavenly Father. Open the ears of your heart and be prepared to record what He reveals to you. The Holy Spirit will cause a verse of scripture to come alive to give you understanding or instruction. The Lord may also give you prayers or scriptures as an effective weapon against the attacks of the devil.

Be sensitive to His leading. Don't be in a hurry, but rather learn to wait on Him so you know His heart's desires for you and those for whom you pray. He will instruct you on how to cultivate the heart and plant the seed of His Word.

The purpose of this manual is to encourage you and give you the tools you will need to hit the mark you are aiming for. But tools alone will be ineffective; in order to see results you must be sensitive to the Holy Spirit. This book is not meant to be a formula, but rather a manual to lead you to press in to the only One who can bring your loved ones home.

> Praying always with all prayer and supplication in the Spirit, and watching thereunto with all perseverance and supplication for all saints ...
> Ephesians 6:18 (KJV)

This message is a compilation of over 20 years of prayer; writing and teaching that we at Garden of the Heart Ministries have learned and walked out in relation to intercession for our wayward loved ones. When God began to deal with me about writing this journal, my children were little. Over the years, I have penned many God-taught lessons that are threaded throughout this work.

Perhaps prayer in the past was boring and tedious for you. Now it can be an exciting adventure as you watch God, the Master Gardener, bring forth His beauty into the hearts of others.

He stands at the garden gate beckoning, calling, "Come in."

Do you hear Him? Hesitate no longer.

Take the first step on your journey into . . . the Garden of the Heart.

Prayer:

Father, soften my heart and cause me to be sensitive to Your voice. Prepare my heart so that I can hear You clearly. Show me how to cultivate my wayward loved ones' hearts through prayer. If that brings me knee deep in mud as You till the soil of their hearts, so be it. I can only do it with the power of Your Holy Spirit. I will not give up! For in due time the harvest WILL come! Amen

Now, spend some time waiting in His presence. Praise Him and thank Him for what He is going to do. Praise Him for who He is. Praise Him that all things are possible with Him. Commit to praying for your wayward loved ones. You must have a plan, or you can be sure that distractions will keep you from this important call.

> ... See that you fulfill the ministry, which you have received in the Lord.
>
> Colossians 4:17 (RSV)

> ... We have seen that the land is very good. Aren't you going to do something? Don't hesitate to go there and take it over.
>
> Judges 18:9

Will you commit today to pray for your wayward loved ones? God so desires to give you what you ask for when it aligns with His will, and He is clear that His will is for your loved ones to return to Him. Go ahead, make the pledge today. I'm praying with you, and that's another of God's promises you can claim right now:

> When two of you get together on anything at all on earth and make a prayer of it, my Father in heaven goes into action.
>
> Matthew 18:19 (MSG)

All God's best to you and your family.

Debra

Mud on My Knees Prayer Pledge

On this day, _____,

I, _____,

commit to pray for and appropriate God's promises for

_____, _____,

_____ on a

_____ basis using the tools in this manual

and God's Word.

16

Pray & Write...

Notes...

"How To" Guide

BLESSED BE the Lord, my Rock and my keen and
firm Strength, Who teaches my hands to war
and my fingers to fight.
Psalm 144:1 (AMP)

Prayer Guide/Journal

*T*his powerful resource is a combination of teaching and prayer journal, filled with:

- Scriptures to pray
- Valuable insights
- Life transforming stories

You can use this guide in several different ways.

- As a Resource or Devotional – read it and pray as God leads you.

- As a Prayer Journal – read it and use it to interact with God, recording His activity in the lives of your loved ones and how He leads you in prayer.

- As a Personal Prayer Garden – use it to cultivate your own opulent garden where God's touch is evident in your life and the lives of your loved ones.

- For a Wayward Loved Ones Prayer Group.

Personal Prayer Garden

*M*UD ON MY KNEES uses five important features in developing a personal prayer garden. Following these steps can lead to a garden filled with the blossoms of answered prayer and God's touch of grace in the hearts of those for whom you are interceding. If you're ready to join the Master Gardener, grab your tool kit and let's get started!

I. DEVOTIONAL ...

This manual has been created as a devotional from which you will gain prayer tools and insights to put into practice. Whenever you see the "SOWING SEEDS" section, it is time to:

1. Receive God's seed-thoughts into your heart,
2. Meditate on them until they take root in your heart, or
3. Sow God's seed into the heart of another through prayer.

Many of the teachings within this work need to be put into practice or it will remain "head" knowledge and you will not bear the fruit that you desire. Therefore, I suggest you go over these truths daily for several months until prayer becomes a way of life. Set a time where you can be alone with God and begin incorporating them into your prayer life. Get in the habit of writing what God reveals. We have provided extra writing pages throughout for you to journal, pray and record those things you want to remember.

II. A PRAYER JOURNAL ...

This book, while available either as an e-book or printed book, is meant to be held in your hands, so you can ponder it, manipulate it and refer back to it without having to fire up any electronic devise. Mark it up – go ahead – you can always start a separate journal if this one gets too love worn! To do it "right," you'll need the following things:

a. **Pen**: Treat yourself to a special pen. Gel pens work well, although you might prefer an expensive, fancy pen. Whatever you decide, make sure it writes well and is comfortable to hold.

b. **Highlighter:** After recording insights that God speaks to your heart, you may want to highlight them so you can easily locate and re-read them later. At times, God speaks to get our attention, to warn us or prepare us for the future. Highlighting will help you discern what He is trying to tell you. Looking back, many times you will notice that He repeats His messages weeks or months apart in order to get your attention. If you do not record it, you might miss what God is doing.

III. JOURNAL PAGES...

Write, therefore, what you have seen, what is now and what will take place later.
Revelation 1:19

One of the most important features in this prayer journal is the capability to use it as a journal where you will write your thoughts, prayers and feelings to the Lord. Journaling might be difficult as you face the hard places your prodigals are traveling, but the insights you receive through this exercise of interaction with the Lord will far outweigh the pain – trust me, I know. As you slow down long enough to hear from God, He will encourage you and fill you with hope. Record whatever God speaks to you in your journaling pages.

Use your Journal section to:

o Keep track of what the Lord reveals to you. God will give you revelations and lead you to pray in ways you would otherwise know nothing about.
o Record scriptures, dreams, visions and insights that He gives you.
o Pour out your concerns and pain about your loved ones.
o Unload your heart to Him.
o Record what you see God doing in your prodigal's life. This will encourage you to press on and not give up.

IV. PRAYER PAGES ...

Sowing and Reaping pages, provide a way to date and record prayer requests and answered prayers, to help you create a legacy of God's faithfulness that can be passed down from generation to generation.

Write out your prayer requests in the "Sowing" column and answers to prayer in the "Reaping" column. I use the Sowing and Reaping forms specifically for my prodigals or my immediate family. Be sure to date every entry in order to keep a record of when and how God answered your prayers. By doing this, a powerful testimony of God's love and faithfulness is imprinted eternally in your wayward loved ones' hearts – and in yours.

Prayer takes commitment. If you will commit to only 15 - 30 minutes a day in prayer, you will see God's movement in your prodigals' lives. As you experience God, 15 minutes will easily turn into an hour. Pray the personalized scriptures in the prayer section. God's Word will not return to Him void. Praying scripture is powerful. His Word is at work in your loved ones' lives. (1Thes. 2:13)

Pray & Write pages have been placed throughout this resource. Fill them with other prayer lists such as ministries, friends or extended family.

Additionally add the names of specific prayer requests next to a scripture promise in the Seed Section of the back of this journal. Don't forget to date it.

Notes pages have been added throughout for you to record additional teaching on spiritual warfare, allowing you to keep everything in one place.

V. ADDITIONAL SCRIPTURE PAGES ...

Add your own personalized scriptures as the Lord directs you. When you are reading your Bible, a verse might jump out at you. Pay attention and **write it DOWN!** God may be trying to encourage you or reveal something to you. Write them out and turn these life-giving seeds into prayer. When we know not what to pray or ask for, God will always lead us to what's needed – in our own lives and the lives of our loved ones.

*Y*ou will notice that throughout this journal, garden terminology is used.

Descriptions of the garden related to God's people and their heart are found threaded throughout the Bible. Within scripture, God uses the "garden" to give us a clear word picture of His relationship with mankind.

Your loved one's heart is His garden and He is asking you to join Him in cultivating, seed planting, watering and, perhaps most importantly, enjoying the harvest. Trust me – NO, trust God – harvest IS coming. So won't you join me in working with the Master Gardener?

> My work was to plant the seed in your hearts, and Apollos' work was to water it, but it was God, not we, who made the garden grow in your hearts. 1 Cor. 3:6 (TLB)

Pray & Write. . .

Their Hearts - Your Garden

*L*onging to see my family reflect Christ, I poured out my heart to the Lord.

"Lord, teach me how to raise my children until they are changed into Your likeness." This was a cry from deep within my heart.

The answer I received to my cries was one that changed our lives forever. Hopefully, it has the same life-affirming impact on you as well. It seemed I could hear God's clear instruction in my spirit. Here is what He spoke to me that day:

- "As in all spiritual things, the battle is won on your knees. Saturate each child in prayer."

- "I have given you a Garden — their Hearts. You are like a gardener and these children, their hearts, are your garden. Pull out the weeds — the fleshly thinking, the world and sin — for they will surely kill the plants."

- "I have given you all you need: My Word and My Spirit. On that last day there will be no excuse, for I have given you all through My Son, Jesus Christ."

- "Fill their hearts with My Word – the seeds of life. Plant it and surely a great harvest shall sprout. Through My Spirit I have provided you with all you need. Plant My Word."

- "Pray, pray, pray!"

- "This prayer brings the water needed for growth. For My Spirit shall be poured upon them and fill them, bringing them to life."

- "Protect your garden from insects — the devil, your enemy. If you do not, he will surely eat away the roots so they will shrivel and die."

- "Plant in their hearts and you will reap a great harvest. Plant! Water through much prayer and the rain of the Holy Spirit shall fall, and surely much fruit shall be produced."

- "Do not allow My garden to lay dormant, for surely the weeds shall strangle the life out of each plant."

- "Pray. Follow the Holy Spirit, for He knows the times for planting, and pulling, watering and sunning. He shall teach you to be the gardener that I have called you to be."

- "Plant so they are exposed to much sun — My SON, Jesus — His Light will stimulate growth. They must learn to search for the Light, for all they need is found in the light. The Son knows how much shade to provide. Do not plant them in darkness, for here, too, they will shrivel and die. Be vigilant in caring for this garden, and you will harvest fruit for eternal life."

Do you long to see your loved ones changed to be more like Christ? Then heed His voice heard in the Bible as well as in your heart, and learn from the Master.

Maybe you've never thought of God as a gardener before, but look closely in scripture and you find Him planting, watering and reaping in the hearts of His people. And don't be intimidated or put off if you're not a gardener yourself. God will teach you how to effectively plant in His garden.

> We are God's garden ... the garden of His delight. 1 Cor. 3:9 (AMP), Isaiah 5:7

From the beginning of time, gardening was in the heart of the Father. Let's look to see the significance that God places on the garden so that we can understand more fully what it means to be a "gardener of the heart." Garden terminology is threaded throughout scripture, in both the Old and New Testaments.

Scriptures are incorporated throughout this book as well as in an expanded, topical section added at the very end of the book, to help you cultivate your family's Scriptural seeds.

Gardening - Old Testament

Throughout the Bible we see God caring for His garden – His people. He is diligently planting, watering, weeding, destroying harmful insects and other garden invaders, and promoting growth in them. You can see from the following scriptures how God tends His garden.

- **HE PLANTED A GARDEN, PUT MAN IN IT**

  Now the LORD God had planted a garden in the east, in Eden; and there he put the man he had formed.   Gen. 2:8

  And the LORD God took the man and put him in the Garden of Eden to tend and guard and keep it.   Gen. 2:15
  (AMP)

- **AND FELLOWSHIPPED WITH HIM THERE**

  Then the man and his wife heard the sound of the LORD God as he was walking in the garden in the cool of the day ...   Gen. 3:8

- **WE ARE HIS GARDEN - THE GARDEN OF HIS DELIGHT**

  The vineyard of the LORD Almighty is the house of Israel, and the men of Judah are the garden of his delight ...   Isa. 5:7

- **SOIL PREPARATION**

  Sow for yourselves righteousness, reap the fruit of unfailing love, and break up your unplowed ground; for it is time to seek the LORD, until he comes and showers righteousness on you.   Hos. 10:12

- **PLANTING**

  I will rejoice in doing them good and will assuredly plant them in this land with all my heart and soul.   Jer. 32:41

- ## WATERING

  The LORD will guide you always; he will satisfy your needs in a sun-scorched land and will strengthen your frame. You will be like a well-watered garden, like a spring whose waters never fail.   Isa. 58:11

  Let us acknowledge the LORD; let us press on to acknowledge him. As surely as the sun rises, he will appear; he will come to us like the winter rains, like the spring rains that water the earth.   Hos. 6:3

  For I will pour water on the thirsty land, and streams on the dry ground; I will pour out my Spirit on your offspring, and my blessing on your descendants. They will spring up like grass in a meadow, like poplar trees by flowing streams. Isa. 44:3-4

- ## LIGHT AND SUNSHINE

  He is like the light of morning at sunrise on a cloudless morning, like the brightness after rain that brings the grass from the earth.   2 Sam. 23:4

  For the Lord God is a sun and shield, he bestows favor and honor. No good thing does the Lord withhold from those who walk uprightly.   Psalm 84:11 (NRSV)

- ## SOWING AND REAPING

  Plant the good seeds of righteousness, and you will reap a crop of my love; plow the hard ground of your hearts, for now is the time to seek the Lord, that He may come and shower salvation upon you.   Hos. 10:12 (TLB)

- ## CAUSING GROWTH

  They shall live again beneath my shadow, they shall flourish as a garden; they shall blossom like the vine, their fragrance shall be like the wine of Lebanon.
  Hos.14: 7 (NRSV)

*Y*our heart was created as a place where God can dwell and have fellowship with you. He chose the image of a garden to illustrate this relationship.

The Father is already at work in His Garden - the Garden of His delight! His people are the apple of His eye! (Ps. 17:8) Now, whether you are an experienced gardener or not, you have the opportunity to join Him as He gardens the hearts of men. Before you can garden in the hearts of others, you must be able to recognize God's cultivation process in your own heart. On a regular basis, take time to become familiar with how He is working in your heart.

SOWING SEEDS

*R*e-read the scriptures in this chapter. Choose one of them and journal how you sense God working in your life. Recording what you see Him doing on a daily basis will help you to recognize the way He cultivates the heart. It all starts with:

Journal: What is God doing in my heart? Is my heart pliable to His hand?

Honesty here will help protect you from a heart that moves away from God.

Pray and Write !

Gardening-New Testament

*I*n the New Testament we see Jesus:

- ## LOVED TO PRAY AND MEET IN THE GARDEN

  And now they came to an olive grove called the Garden of Gethsemane, and he instructed his disciples, "Sit here, while I go and pray."   Mark 14:32 (TLB)

- ## WAS BETRAYED IN A GARDEN

  When Jesus had spoken these words, He went forth with His disciples over the ravine of the Kidron, where there was a garden, into which He Himself entered, and His disciples. Now Judas also, who was betraying Him, knew the place; for Jesus had often met there with His disciples.   John 18:1-2 (NASB)

- ## WAS CRUCIFIED IN A GARDEN

  Now in the place where He was crucified there was a garden; and in the garden a new tomb, in which no one had yet been laid.   John 19:41 (NASB)

*T*he garden played an important role in God's plan to save mankind. Jesus loved to pray and meet with His disciples in a garden. He yielded His will to take our place in payment for sin in the garden on the Mount of Olives. There, through the agony of prayer, Jesus surrendered His life for the redemption of mankind.

The ransom price was paid in full as the sins of the world were taken freely and carried by Christ on the cross. His mutilated body was buried in a tomb, sealed with a large stone. But death held the Savior only three days and nights in its icy grip.

When God raised Jesus from the dead with the dynamite power of the Holy Spirit, Jesus was then seated far above all rule and authority, power and dominion. All things were put in subjection under Him (Eph. 1:20-22). Jesus made a public display of the enemy, totally stripping him of power and triumphing over him (Col. 2:15).

No longer was man forced to bow to Satan, the god of this earth. The King of Kings had taken His rightful place. Man once again had free access to the Father through Jesus, the Son.

With His blood, Jesus bought your wayward loved ones back for God and purchased their freedom from slavery. When they ask His forgiveness, He becomes their Savior and removes the handcuffs and chains of sin, delivering them from the dark domain. They are freed! Now, they are God's own property, sealed with His Holy Spirit.

You must be vigilant, however, and shield their heart against the lies of the deceiver, for he will try to trespass and reclaim lost territory. Standing on God's promises will enable you to stop him cold so that your prodigals will walk joyously in the freedom Christ has given them.

> It is for freedom that Christ has set us free. Stand firm, then, and do not let yourselves be burdened again by a yoke of slavery.　　　Galatians 5:1

A trespasser is one who enters unlawfully upon the land of another. Satan is no longer the landowner of the garden of the heart. Do not allow him to trespass! Apply the blood and use the Name of Jesus by which he has been defeated.

Do you see your loved ones dabbling in sin? Are they allowing the deceiver to come into the garden of their hearts? Then stand up and use the tools that God has given you and **take back the land the enemy has stolen!** While you are taking back the land, at times you might notice other captives. Snatch whomever you can along the way and take them with you.

When the teen years came, I noticed the enemy trying to trespass. As I read my Bible, Proverbs 6:30-31 jumped out at me and I knew that I was supposed to use this verse in prayer.

> Men do not despise a thief, if he steals to satisfy his soul when he is hungry; but if he be found, he shall restore sevenfold…　　　Proverbs 6:30-31 (KJV)

Some scriptures are not promises but principles. Others, the Lord will quicken to you when you are reading them and He will make them personal.

I prayed, "In the Name of Jesus, the thief has been found out and must release seven of my children's friends." I then continued to pray for their salvation on a regular basis.

A few months later my daughter's friend, Sarah, was kicked out of her home and asked if she could live with us. Within the first two weeks I shared the gospel with her and she gave her heart to the Lord. One Saturday morning, she awakened me and asked, "I have to work today, but can three of my friends come over? They want you to tell them about Jesus."

I said, "YES!"... a resounding YES!

At 1:00 p.m. there was a knock on my door. Sarah's friends, Mary and Tom, arrived. After sharing with them, they knelt on my living room floor and gave their hearts to Jesus. As we prayed, there was another knock on the door. It was their friend, Jim. When he entered, Mary and Tom said, "Can you pray for him? We want him to feel what we felt!" They felt the presence of God and wanted Jim to experience the same thing.

I said, "Wait, let's talk to him first." So I shared the gospel once more and he gave his heart to the Lord. I now had three teenagers kneeling on my living room floor giving their hearts to Jesus. God showed up in an amazing way and the enemy had to release them. Within the next year, I had the opportunity to lead three more of my children's friends to the Lord – all seven I had put on my list and prayed for diligently.

SOWING SEEDS

*G*od answers prayer! So don't give up. Be sensitive to His leading and follow Him as you snatch hearts back for God.

Not only can you take their hearts back for God, but be sensitive to the leading of the Holy Spirit and take all who are ripe for the harvest with them!

> Save some by snatching them as from the very flames of hell itself. And as for others, help them to find the Lord by being kind to them, but be careful that you yourselves aren't pulled along into their sins. Hate every trace of their sin while being merciful to them as sinners. Jude 23 (TLB)

Father, help me to be sensitive to your Spirit. Widen my vision to see others who are ripe for harvest as I focus on my prodigals.

Prayer Journal:

It's time to get your knees muddy! List the names of your loved ones, prodigals or even the lost that you can start praying for in your prayer journal.

Create a prayer page for yourself as well. As you pray for others, God will be cultivating your heart.

Notes...

Cultivation Process

My Word ... shall not return to Me void, but it shall accomplish
that which I please and purpose, and it shall prosper in
the thing for which I sent it.
Isaiah 55:11

Pray & Write. . .

Gardening the Heart

Now that we know the significance God places on the garden, let's read what the Bible says about cultivating and seed planting in the hearts of man as well. The first garden is symbolic of a spiritual garden – the heart. Just as God gave Adam the responsibility of tilling and keeping the Garden of Eden, He gives you the responsibility of keeping the garden of the heart.

To "keep" in the Hebrew means "to watch and to guard." Adam was to watch and guard his garden. But Adam wasn't paying close attention. He allowed Satan to invade the Garden of Eden. Deception entered his wife's heart and Adam soon fell into disobedience, losing the land that God gave them. (Gen. 3)

Let's learn from Adam's mistakes and guard our gardens – our loved ones' hearts – from the enemy's intrusion; and reclaim the land through prayer, cultivating it until it flourishes once again.

Apostle Paul understood the concept of gardening the hearts of others. He knew how to co-labor with God in the garden of the heart. This is why he labored through His prayers and preached until Christ was completely formed (molded) in people.

> My little children, for whom I labor in birth again until Christ is formed in you.   Galatians 4:19 (NKJV)

Even though the Lord made each personality unique from others, He desires each person's heart to take on the character of His Son.

> … He destined you from the beginning … to be molded into the image of His Son (and share inwardly His likeness).   Romans 8:29 (AMP)

Apostle Paul said,

> My work was to plant the seed in your hearts, and Apollos' work was to water it, but it was God, not we, who made the garden grow in your hearts.   1 Corinthians 3:6 (TLB)

According to the Vines Expository Dictionary, the "heart" stands for the inner being of man, the man himself. As such, it is the fountain of all he does (Prov. 4:23). All his thoughts, desires, words, and actions flow from deep within him. Yet a man cannot understand his own "heart." (Jer. 17:9) As a man goes on in his own way, his "heart" becomes harder and harder. But God will circumcise (cut away the uncleanness of) the heart of His people, so they will love and obey Him with their whole being (Deut. 30:6)[1].

In the Old Testament, the Hebrew definition for "heart" refers to the total person, encompassing his inner life and character. If you look closely throughout scripture you will find that it includes our emotions, perceptions, thoughts, understanding, reasoning, conscience, intentions, motive, will and imagination. In the New Testament, the Greek defines the word, "heart" as the place where understanding, reasoning powers, conscience, motive, will and imagination reside. Your heart is who you are; the center of man's existence. You could say, it is the meeting place of soul and spirit.

Let's co-labor together with God and pray for our loved ones until their hearts are formed into the image of Christ, for then they will bear much fruit. It is in their heart where God reveals Himself and deals with them. This is where relationship happens.

The heart is also the place where Satan attacks, trying to infiltrate in an effort to cut off relationship with the Lord.

There is a very real battle going on for the hearts of men and woman. You can see it just by turning on the television. We are constantly inundated through media filled with lust, greed, pride, hate, murder and deceptions of all kinds, desensitizing our hearts.

It is not sufficient to pray only when you feel like it. You must set a watch over their hearts and fast and pray until their hearts are softened and turned back to God. As you persist in prayer, God's power will be released and their hearts will begin to soften once again.

God places great importance on the heart. He created our hearts and put it within man so that He could fellowship with us there. He is always watching.

> From the place of his habitation he looketh upon all the inhabitants of the earth. He fashioned their hearts …
> He considereth all their works.   Psalm 33:14-15 (KJV)

He expects us to be keepers of the heart. Scriptures tell us to guard our hearts above all else!

> Above all else, guard your heart, for it affects everything you do.
>   Proverbs 4:23 (NLT)

---

1 *From Vine's Expository Dictionary of Biblical Words, Copyright© 1985, Thomas Nelson Publishers.*

SOWING SEEDS

*T*he word "heart" is mentioned more than 800 times in the Bible. If God puts such importance on the heart, we should too.

Prayer Journal:

If you haven't already, go to your prayer journal and create a page for each of your loved ones. You will find categorized scriptures under the "Seed Section." Write out scriptures that are specific to them in the sowing column of your journal. Keep your Bible in hand. Many times the Holy Spirit will quicken a verse of scripture to you, to either edify or instruct you. Otherwise, He may bring it to you as a weapon to wield in prayer against the forces of darkness as you take hold of His already accomplished victory. Be sensitive to His leading. Do not be in a hurry; rather, learn to wait on Him.

Pray and Write!

Pray & Write. . .

Aim for the Heart

*H*ave you prayed for your loved one's return, yet they seem more distant than ever? Possibly, you are aiming your prayers in the wrong direction. Take your eyes off their **outward** appearance and circumstances, and aim your prayers towards their **heart**.

> … God sees not as man sees, for man looks at the outward appearance, but the LORD looks at the heart.　　　　1 Samuel 16:7 (NASB)

If God looks at the heart, we should too! How do you aim your prayers for the heart?

For years I had been guarding my son's heart through prayer. But when he was a teenager, he brought a young woman home and I could see that his heart was clearly in danger of being invaded by worldly temptations.

Just as any other mother, I was ready to rush in, defend and fight for my son. Images of me with my old worn spade in hand, ready to attack and yank out this female weed, as I perceived her, danced in my head. Thank God I stopped to pray, though my heart was filled with a mixture of grief and anger. "Oh God, please remove her from his life for she will quickly destroy what you have helped me cultivate."

The Lord's tender response was not what I expected. "I could remove her, but he will only be attracted to another just like her. She is not the problem. The problem is his heart. Aim for the heart!"

Enlightened, I opened my Bible:

> The king's heart is like channels of water in the hand of the Lord; He turns it wherever He wishes.　　　　Proverbs 21:1 (NASB)

Surrendering, I prayed, "Lord, I place his heart in Your hands. Turn it toward Your will and away from her."

I then searched through my Bible and found many promises from God's Word related to the heart. I prayed other scriptures, such as:

Lord, You promised to circumcise his heart (Deut. 30:6) and open it to the gospel; and remove all hindrances so he can obey Your truth. I claim that promise right now.

Thank You, Father, that You have given him a new heart and put a new spirit within him; and that You will take away his heart of stone and give him a heart of flesh. I believe Your Word that says You will put Your Spirit within him and cause him to walk in Your statutes, and to keep Your judgments and do them. (Ezek. 36:26-27 NKJ)

Thank You, Lord for giving him a heart to know You, for then he will return to You with his whole heart. (Jer. 24:7 NASB)

I poured over scriptures like these daily, believing God to soften and change his heart. Many days passed as I continued to pour out my heart to the Lord, lifting my hands to Him for the life of my young son. I was comforted in remembering that those who sow in tears reap with songs of joy. (Ps. 126:5-6)

The seed of God's Word that was planted in my son's heart was growing; and I soon noticed that the young woman (who had such need of prayer herself, and who had attempted to uproot the good seed in my son's heart) was gone, never to return!

That day, God taught me one of the most valuable lessons that I have learned about prayer: Aim for the Heart!

We can aim our prayers at circumstances, and we should, **if** God leads us to. But it is much more effective to aim them toward the heart. Your prayers will soften your loved ones' hearts, so they can hear the voice of God and turn away from their sin.

If you aim your prayers directly towards the heart, you will see answers more quickly. Why? Circumstances may change, but unless the heart changes, it is likely that your prodigals will repeat their past choices.

When praying for someone else's heart, it is their decision to respond, but your prayers will open the door for the Holy Spirit to cultivate and soften their heart. Praying daily will cause hearts to be more receptive to God's voice. Then you can effectively zero in on the other promises they need for their situations.

Are your loved ones entangled in sin? Is the enemy deceiving them?

> "...do not be afraid of the enemy; [earnestly] remember the Lord and imprint Him [on your minds], great and terrible, and [take from Him courage to] fight for your brethren, your sons, your daughters, your wives, and your homes.
> Nehemiah 4:14 (AMP)

SOWING SEEDS

*U*sually, underneath all the outward layers of rebellion, anger, bitterness, and pride is a person hungering to be loved, healed and accepted. Sometimes the layers are so thick that they cannot admit their need, for they can't see it anymore. But your prayers will help remove some of those layers so that they can see the truth, "and the truth will set them free." (John 8:32)

This is accomplished through prayer that is aimed toward the heart. As you learn how to pray God's promises over your loved one's hearts, little by little you will recover the ground the enemy has stolen. You do not have to struggle to get the victory. Jesus has already given you the victory through His sacrifice at Calvary.

> ... We have seen that the land is very good. Aren't you going to do something? Don't hesitate to go there and take it over. Judges 18:9

Before you go in, take a moment on your knees and scout out the land of their heart. Ask the Lord to reveal how to pray. He is the only One who knows the hearts of all men.

> ... for you alone know the hearts of all men.   1 Kings 8:39

Be sensitive to His voice.

> The Lord Himself goes before you ...   Deuteronomy 31:8

As you assess the land, it is important to keep your focus on Jesus. As you do, He will reveal how He wants you to pray. Remain in an intimate relationship with Him and walk in the light, and He will reveal darkness.

Personalize and pray the following scriptures:

> The LORD your God will circumcise your hearts and the hearts of your descendants, so that you may love him with all your heart and with all your soul, and live.   Deuteronomy 30:6

> I will give you a new heart and put a new spirit in you; I will remove from you your heart of stone and give you a heart of flesh. And I will put my Spirit in you and move you to follow my decrees and be careful to keep my laws.   Ezekiel 36:26-27

I will give them a heart to know me, that I am the LORD. They will be my people, and I will be their God, for they will return to me with all their heart.

Jeremiah 24:7

Journal:

Now write a prayer to God, thanking Him for what He is doing in the hearts of your wayward loved ones.

Prayer Journal:

If God reveals anything to you while praying, write it in the sowing column of the person you are praying for. Keep this between you, God and your prayer partner. This information is not for you to broadcast. Be faithful with the assignments that God gives you and He will give you more.

Soil Preparation

The farmer plants the Word. Some people are like the seed that falls on the hardened soil of the road. No sooner do they hear the Word than Satan snatches away what has been planted in them.   Mark 4:14-15 (MSG)

*I*f there is one element that is essential to all beautiful gardens, it is healthy, fertile soil. Good garden soil is rarely found waiting for you, but it can be developed with the right tools.

As with any garden, the garden of the heart also needs soft, pliable soil if it is to bear fruit that will delight the Lord. If the soil of your loved ones' hearts remains rock hard, the seed won't take root and the enemy will snatch it away. After years of being trampled on, like soil, the heart can become very compact and hardened. That is why Jesus warned us not to let our hearts become calloused to His voice. (Matt. 13:15, Heb. 3:15)

Hard hearts are conducive to growing weeds. Therefore, it is important that the soil of the heart remain soft. Not only is hard soil conducive to growing weeds, but have you ever noticed how difficult it is to kneel on earth that is cracked and baked hard as brick? I am pretty sure you will agree with me when I say, "My knees HURT!" Right? Well, in a similar way, when kneeling in the garden of hardened hearts, it isn't always comfortable; your heart may ache, you will be heavily burdened and easily brought to tears – I know, I've been there and felt all the heartache. But there is hope. In an earthly garden in springtime, the frost brings rocks to the surface so that they can be dislodged. In a spiritual garden, as you pray, the Lord unearths these hardened areas in His time. God is calling you to join Him in this work!

> Parched ground that soaks up the rain and then produces an abundance of carrots and corn for its gardener gets God's "Well done!" ...   Hebrews 6:7 (MSG)

So let's get serious with our faces to the ground, no matter how long it takes and pray, pray, pray. God promises to take away our stony hearts and give us hearts that are pliable and soft! (Ez. 36:26)

When God taught me to pray scripture promises to soften the heart, I prayed them daily, not only over my family's hearts, but my own heart as well. I prayed persistently, even though I did not see much happen at first. Doing so was like opening the garden gate and inviting Him to do what He said He would do. Little by little I could see changes here and there, so I continued to plant these heart seeds, thanking Him for His promises. Several years passed and I was still holding on to the seeds of His promise, planting them into our hearts.

About this time my husband, Geno, fell into depression. I could see that he had some heavy things in his heart. So I asked my Pastor to see him. Our Pastor agreed to see him, but in his wisdom, suggested I come along. Before the first session, I ran into him in the church office.

He said, "I want to warn you, this may be very difficult, for you, for Geno, and for me because I am going to ask you some questions and I am not sure how you will take them." Not realizing that I also had some hardened areas in my heart, I willingly agreed. Unknown to me, the Lord was getting ready to unearth those hardened areas of stuffed pain that I had buried so many years before.

But, praise the Lord, "What God reveals, He heals!"

During the first session, our pastor turned and asked me to tell him about my mother. As I began to share about her death when I was a young girl, I started to cry.

He asked, "This seems awfully fresh, have you ever grieved her death?"

"Yes," I quickly answered. As I left, I turned to him and stated, "This wasn't so bad."

He said, "Oh, this is nothing yet. We're just getting started."

I went to the ladies room and looked up, "God, what is he going to ask me?" Immediately I could hear God's gentle voice questioning me. "Is there anything you do not want to talk about?"

"Yes." I answered. He reminded me that I had never grieved my mother's death and I had never shared with anyone regarding an assault that occurred when I was a teenager.

Well you can be pretty sure I put on my running shoes and declared that I would never go back to counseling. Up to five times a day, I wrote in my journal, "I refuse to go back. I will never go back into that office!" Why was I struggling so hard? The Holy Spirit was bringing all of the pain I had denied for so long to the surface of my heart, and it HURT! There was a reason I buried it so long ago, I didn't want to face it. But, God was beginning to heal me and I soon discovered I could not outrun God. He was right there keeping up with me the whole time. After all, He was faithfully answering my prayers, although I didn't know it at the time. All week long He brought Psalm 139 to my heart in the form of a song. "Where can you go from My Spirit, where can you hide from My eyes?"

I knew that He was asking me to surrender to His hand. So I went back and as I did, God dislodged the obstacles of pain I acquired in my youth. For the first time, I grieved my parents' deaths as if it happened yesterday. One by one, He dealt with pain and offenses and healed me physically, emotionally and spiritually. He waited until the time was right. He healed my husband's heart as well. His plans for us were plans to prosper us, not to harm us, plans to give us hope and a future, making our hearts suitable for new life to spring forth.

> ...For I will pour water on the thirsty ground and send streams coursing through the parched earth. I will pour my Spirit into your descendants and my blessing on your children. They shall sprout like grass on the prairie, like willows by flowing streams.
>
> Isaiah 44:3-4 (MSG)

SOWING SEEDS

*H*is plans for your prodigals are plans to give them hope, a future and an expected end! (Jeremiah 29:11)

As you pray, He will cultivate the hearts of your loved ones as well. Like a farmer, you may not see what is happening deep beneath the soil, but you can be assured that God is answering your prayers and that He is at work. It takes time. Sometimes you will see results rather quickly and at other times you may not see any visible signs for quite a while. So if nothing is visible immediately, do not give up. God is at work deep beneath the soil of their hearts. In due time you will reap!

Prayer Journal:

Go to the scripture area in the back of this journal and pray (daily) the Heart Scriptures on pages 163 – 165 over the hearts of your prodigals. You are in a covenant relationship with God. You can believe His promises to change the hearts of your loved ones.

_____
_____
_____
_____
_____
_____
_____
_____
_____
_____
_____
_____
_____
_____
_____

Pray and Write!

Digging Up Rocks

$\mathcal{B}$uried rocks are those things that are hidden below the surface of the heart, hard things that are not easy to deal with. These things can weigh you down and obstruct the growth that God is aiming for. They will be continual stumbling stones. The Lord knows all about these painful, hidden secrets of your prodigals' lives and He wants them to be free of them. He does not want the enemy to use them to build an inroad into their heart or a barrier that would keep God out.

GOD'S Cultivation

$\mathcal{S}$o don't let a few rocks in the garden path stop you! God can unearth them.

But as you proceed in the cultivation process, let me give you a word of advice. There is a difference between looking for rocks yourself, and allowing God to reveal them in His own time. This is a work <u>only</u> God can do, all in His own gentle way. It is not your responsibility to plow into your loved one's heart every time you see an obstacle. Be careful here or, you might plant a seed of bitterness, as my friend Tom did.

Tom was a new Christian and was zealous for the Lord. He loved His daughter, Carrie, with all of his heart. Over the years he watched her faith growing strong in the Lord. As a good Christian parent, he ensured that she attended Sunday school, youth group and even a Christian school.

Carrie gave her heart to the Lord when she was seven years old. Tom had big hopes for his little girl. He wanted her to make a difference in this world. But as Carrie reached her teen years, she was curious about the things of the world and snuck off to worldly dances, began wearing lots of makeup and hung around with the wrong crowd. It was Tom's responsibility to watch over her and guide her in the things of the Lord, and rightfully so; God expected that of him.

But Tom's disappointment led to harsh words and a hardening of his heart towards his daughter. Deep within his heart a root of bitterness was growing as he pondered, "How could she turn from the things that I spent years teaching her?"

As in earthly gardens, weeds have no property lines and before long this weed of bitterness crept straight into Carrie's heart, choking out much of the seed that was sown in previous years. Her heart hardened and she decided to have nothing to do with Christianity.

As you intercede for your prodigal, be mindful that it is your responsibility to pray and God's to change hearts. As you parent your children and even after they are grown, guard your heart from anger and bitterness because they are weeds that spread easily. Always remember, weeds love to root themselves in rocky, hardened ground.

> ... Keep a sharp eye out for weeds of bitter discontent. A thistle or two gone to seed can ruin a whole garden in no time.   Hebrews 12:15 (MSG)

We must be wise in our dealing with our prodigals. "Wisdom" in the Greek is, "one who knows how to regulate his course in view of the movements of God." Find out how God is moving in your prodigal's life and adjust your actions and prayers accordingly. True wisdom is always accompanied with meekness and gentleness (James 3:13).

> Father, show me how You are working in my prodigal's life so that I can join You in what you are doing. Help me to be quick to hear, slow to speak and slow to be angry. (James 1:19)

Cultivating Your Heart

> O Lord, you have examined my heart and know everything about me.
> Psalm 139:1 (TLB)

*B*efore you cultivate the hearts of others, focus on your own heart so that you can hear Him clearly.

At salvation, God cleansed you from your sins. Yet you need daily cleansing because sin can block your communication with God. If you don't confess the sin in your heart, the Lord will not hear you. (Psalm 66:18)

Prayer Journal:

- Stop for a moment and ask God to reveal your heart to you and to forgive you for anything that He brings to your attention.
- Journal what God speaks to your heart and write out your response.
- Do this daily.

Be sensitive to the conviction of the Holy Spirit. When He reveals sin to you, ask Him to forgive you and immediately turn from it. Fill your heart with God's Word so that He can bring it to your remembrance as needed. The concepts within this journal will work effectively in keeping your own heart soft and tender to the Lord. When you sense the Lord at work revealing hardened areas of your own heart, yield to His hand and don't even give it another thought; don't you dare hang on to them! Your harvest is at stake! Clear the rubble from your heart so that nothing will obstruct growth.

The battle for your loved ones' hearts will not be won just because you repeat a few prayers. It comes as you connect your heart with the One who knows the future and has already won the victory. He will give you insight into your prodigal's heart and life so that you can join Him in what He is doing. You do not battle alone. God goes before you!

SOWING SEEDS

*I*f you have failed in your prodigal's life and stumbled over a few stones, remember – God's mercies are new every morning. He can restore what the locusts have eaten! (Joel 2:25 KJV) Today is a new beginning. Pray about restoring your relationship with your loved one. Ask God to reveal what is in your heart and what steps you will need to take to bring healing. This can be a very difficult step to take, but it is the first step to restoration and possibly the first step towards your loved one's return. Let go of past hurts and start planting seeds towards eternity.

> ... On your knees and pray for harvest hands!   Matthew 9:38 (MSG)

Prayer Journal:

Write what God reveals in your journal. Pray until your heart is right before God.

> ... Plow your unplowed fields, but then don't plant weeds in the soil! Yes, circumcise your lives for God's sake. Plow your unplowed hearts ...
> Jeremiah 4:3 (MSG)

> Search me, O God, and know my heart: try me, and know my thoughts: And see if there be any wicked way in me, and lead me in the way everlasting.   Psalm 139:23-24 (KJV)

> If I had cherished sin in my heart, the Lord would not have listened; but God has surely listened and heard my voice in prayer.   Psalm 66:18-19

If we confess our sins, he is faithful and just and will forgive us our sins and purify us from all unrighteousness.   1 John 1:9

He will turn the hearts of the fathers to their children, and the hearts of the children to their fathers…   Malachi 4:6

And now, God, do it again – bring rains to our drought-stricken lives. So those who planted their crops in despair will shout, "Hurrah," at the harvest. So those who went off with heavy hearts will come home laughing with armloads of blessings.
                    Psalm 126:4-6 (MSG)

A Backslidden Heart

For Israel slideth back as a **backsliding** heifer; now the LORD will feed them as a lamb in a large place.   Hosea 4:16 (KJV)

A prodigal is someone who has turned away from God and left his or her first love for Him. At the root of a backslidden heart is a hardened heart. The heart is where you become who you are. This is why you are told in Prov. 4:23 (MSG) to guard your heart with all diligence, for it determines the course of your life. A hardened heart is no longer sensitive to the voice of God and has become spiritually dull. Jesus himself described people whose hearts had become dull and calloused:

> Or this people's heart has become calloused; they hardly hear with their ears, and they have closed their eyes. Otherwise they might see with their eyes, hear with their ears ... understand with their hearts and turn, and I would heal them.   Matthew 13:15

Scripture gives us a window into the heart of backsliders:

> But I have this [one charge to make] against you: that you have left (abandoned) the love that you had at first [you have deserted Me, your first love]. Remember then from what heights you have fallen. Repent (change the inner man to meet God's will) and do the works you did previously [when first you knew the Lord], or else I will visit you and remove your lampstand from its place, unless you change your mind and repent.   Revelation 2:4-5 (AMP)

Biblical Descriptions of a Backslidden Heart

*T*he word "backsliding" in the Hebrew means, "To turn away, to be morally obstinate, rebellious, a revolter, to slide back, to be stubborn and to withdraw." Throughout scripture we see different examples of people whose hearts were backslidden. Let's take a look a look at a few of them.

King Solomon's Backslidden Condition:

> The LORD became angry with Solomon because his heart had turned
> away from the LORD, the God of Israel, who had appeared to him twice.
>
> 1 Kings 11:9

The People of Israel:

> Although our sins testify against us, O LORD, do something for the sake
> of your name. For our backsliding is great; we have sinned against you.
>
> Jeremiah 14:7

Left their First Love:

> "But I have this complaint against you. You don't love me or each other as
> you did at first! Look how far you have fallen! Turn back to me and do the
> works you did at first. If you don't repent, I will come and remove your
> lampstand from its place among the churches. Revelation 2:4-5 (NLT)

Forgot God:

> Yet my people have forgotten me; they burn incense to worthless idols,
> which made them stumble in their ways and in the ancient paths. They
> made them walk in bypaths and on roads not built up. Jeremiah 18:15

Departed From the Faith:

> The Spirit clearly says that in later times some will abandon the faith and
> follow deceiving spirits and things taught by demons. 1 Timothy 4:1

Salt:

> You are the salt of the earth. But if the salt loses its saltiness, how can it
> be made salty again? It is no longer good for anything, except to be
> thrown out and trampled by men.   Matthew 5:13

*R*emember when you first came to the Lord? You thought nothing could ever turn you away from God. But sin can creep in very subtly and our hearts can become hardened. Scripture gives several examples of strong men and women of God who slid away. Even though God appeared to Solomon twice, his heart still turned away from God.

> The LORD became angry with Solomon because his heart had turned
> away from the LORD, the God of Israel, who had appeared to him twice.
>
> 1 Kings 11:9

King David is another example. Let's take a closer look at his backslidden condition to get a full picture of what happens to a person, even a strong Christian, when they move away from following God. After all, God called David, "A man after His own heart."

King David's backsliding began when he was idle in fulfilling his responsibilities. All of the men went off to war, but King David stayed behind. His palace was near the women's bathhouse and when he noticed beautiful Bathsheba bathing, he desired her. So, against his better judgment, he sent for her. This led to adultery, resulting in an unintended pregnancy. When David was informed that Bathsheba was carrying his child, he sent her husband to the front line so he would be killed and his own sin would be covered up. The king's sins were multiple: lust, covetousness of someone else's wife, seduction, adultery, murder, and abuse of power. No wonder "the thing that David had done displeased the Lord." (2 Sam. 11:27)

Even though King David was called a man after God's own heart, when this man of God sinned by allowing his heart to lust after a woman, he quickly backslid away from his first love.

Sin distorted his judgment and he went from a heart that followed after God to a backslidden condition. This spiral down can happen to anyone. We must guard our hearts and the hearts of our loved ones!

As you read the scriptures below, ask God to show you if any of these have led to your loved ones backsliding.

Deception

> But be doers of the Word [obey the message], and not merely listeners to it, betraying yourselves [into deception by reasoning contrary to the Truth].
> James 1:22 (AMP)

> The Spirit clearly says that in later times some will abandon the faith and follow deceiving spirits and things taught by demons. 1 Timothy 4:1

> Dear friends, I urge you, as aliens and strangers in the world, to abstain from sinful desires, which war against your soul.   1 Peter 2:11

Thought life

> … It is the thought-life that pollutes. For from within, out of men's hearts, come evil thoughts of lust, theft, murder, adultery, wanting what belongs to others, wickedness, deceit, lewdness, envy, slander, pride, and all other folly. All these vile things come from within; they are what pollute you and make you unfit for God.   Mark 7:20-23 (TLB)

> Temptation is the pull of man's own evil thoughts and wishes. These evil thoughts lead to evil actions and afterwards to the death penalty from God.   James 1:14-15 (TLB)

> For as he thinketh in his heart, so is he…   Proverbs 23:7 (KJV)

Clean Conscience

Cling tightly to your faith in Christ and always keep your conscience clear, doing what you know is right. For some people have disobeyed their consciences and have deliberately done what they knew was wrong. It isn't surprising that soon they lost their faith in Christ after defying God like that.   1 Timothy 1:19-20 (TLB)

Greed - Coveting

No one can serve two masters. Either he will hate the one and love the other, or he will be devoted to the one and despise the other. You cannot serve both God and Money.   Matthew 6:24

Wickedness

Because of the increase of wickedness, the love of most will grow cold. Matthew 24:12-13

So, because you are lukewarm -- neither hot nor cold -- I am about to spit you out of my mouth.   Revelation 3:16

Pride

When I fed them, they were satisfied; when they were satisfied, they became proud; then they forgot me.   Hosea 13:6

Pride goes before destruction and haughtiness before a fall.
                                              Proverbs 16:18 (TLB)

Disobedience

Then the word of the LORD came to Samuel, "I am grieved that I have made Saul king, because he has turned away from me and has not carried out my instructions." Samuel was troubled, and he cried out to the LORD all that night.   1 Samuel 15:10-11

Bad Friendships

Do not be misled: "Bad Company corrupts good character."
                                              1 Corinthians 15:33

Unbelief

Beware then of your own hearts, dear brothers, lest you find that they, too, are evil and unbelieving and are leading you away from the living God.
                                              Hebrews 3:12 (TLB)

Was King David a wicked man? No, God called him a man after His own heart. (Acts 13:22)

Yet when he did not keep his heart pure, sin crept in and caused him to move from his close relationship with the Lord. When he was confronted with his sin, he repented and God forgave him, although he suffered the consequence. (2 Sam. 12)

Your prodigals have allowed sin to creep in and, little by little, their heart turned away from God. But there is hope. If there is one thing I have learned, it is "do not underestimate God!" He can soften the hardest of hearts! Nothing is impossible with Him! (Luke 1:37) Even though you might recognize the above conditions of the heart in your prodigal's life, God can break through and open their eyes so they can see and be set free!

SOWING SEEDS

*7*he above verses give us a window into some of the things in our prodigals'

lives that may have led them away from the Lord. Record what God reveals on their prayer page. Do not use these scriptures as a weapon to try to convict them of their sin. God will do the convicting. Rather, pray asking God to soften their heart and root it out.

Prayer Journal:

Write the scriptures that relate to them on their prayer page and then pray something like this daily.

Heavenly Father, in Jesus' name, thank You that _____ is a doer of the Word and will obey its message. Open her/his eyes to see the truth. Protect her/him from deception. (James 1:22) I ask that You would remove evil thoughts, sexual immorality, theft, murder, adultery, greed, malice, wickedness, deceit, lewdness, envy, slander, pride, arrogance and all other folly from _____'s heart. (Mark 7:20-23)

Help _____ to keep her/his conscience clear, doing what she/he knows is right. For some people have disobeyed their consciences and have deliberately done what they knew was wrong and have lost their faith in Christ. (1 Timothy 1:19-20)

Remove bad friendships from _____'s life so that she/he will not be misled: for "Bad Company corrupts good character." (1 Corinthians 15:33)

Protect _____'s heart from unbelief that will lead him/her away from You. (Hebrews 3:12)

Pray & Write...

How to Return

*I*f you are reading this and discover that you are the person who is backslidden, you see your own heart being described; there is a remedy for you as well. You can return to the Lord:

And now, Israel, what does the Lord your God require of you but [reverently] to fear the Lord your God, [that is] to walk in all His ways, and to love Him, and to serve the Lord your God with all your [mind and] heart and with your entire being.   Deut. 10:12 (AMP)

➢ CLEANSE YOUR HEART

Therefore, cleanse your sinful hearts and stop your stubbornness.

Deut. 10:16 (TLB)

➢ ACKNOWLEDGE THAT YOU HAVE SINNED

Only acknowledge your guilt; admit that you rebelled against the Lord your God and committed adultery against him by worshiping idols under every tree; confess that you refused to follow me. O sinful children, come home, for I am your Master, and I will bring you again to the land of Israel - one from here and two from there, wherever you are scattered.

Jer. 3:13, 14 (TLB)

➢ REPENT

Repent (change the inner man to meet God's will) and do the works you did previously [when first you knew the Lord], or else I will visit you and remove your lampstand from its place, unless you change your mind and repent.   Rev. 2:5 (AMP)

➢ PRAY

For I know my transgressions, and my sin is always before me. Against you, you only, have I sinned and done what is evil in your sight ...
Psalm 51:3-4

➤ CHANGE YOUR WAYS

> If you return to the Almighty, you will be restored: If you remove wickedness far from your tent.   Job 22:23

> For you, O Lord, are good and forgiving, abounding in steadfast love to all who call on you.   Psalm 86:5 (NRSV)

If you have prayed the above scriptures, God forgives you and you can begin over for,

> As far as the east is from the west, so far has He removed our transgressions from us.   Psalm 103:12

> It is of the LORD's mercies that we are not consumed, because his compassions fail not. They are new every morning: great is thy faithfulness.   Lam. 3:22, 23 (KJV)

> Don't be misled: No one makes a fool of God. What a person plants, he will harvest. The person who plants selfishness, ignoring the needs of others—ignoring God!—harvests a crop of weeds. All he'll have to show for his life is weeds! But the one who plants in response to God, letting God's Spirit do the growth work in him, harvests a crop of real life, eternal life.   Gal. 6:7 (MSG)

God loves you with an everlasting love and welcomes you with open arms!

> … In simple humility, let our gardener, God, landscape you with the Word, making a salvation garden of your life.   James 1:21 (MSG)

A HARD HEART

*W*hen you are ministering to your wayward loved ones, you might be asking yourself, why can't they understand truth? Why don't they comprehend what I'm trying to tell them? They are so blind! It's so simple, you think. Why don't they get it?

Before someone comes to know the Lord, they have a veil over their eyes and they cannot see clearly.

> And even if our gospel is veiled, it is veiled to those who are perishing in whose case the god of this world has blinded the minds of the unbelieving, that they might not see the light of the gospel of the glory of Christ, who is the image of God.   2 Cor. 4:3-4 (NASB)

The word "veiled" in the Greek means, "to hide, cover up, and wrap around." It also means, "To make blind and to dull the intellect." Unbelievers do not see or understand the gospel because they cannot see it. They think that their beliefs are right.

At salvation, this veil is removed.

> But whenever anyone turns to the Lord, the veil is taken away.
> 2 Cor. 3:16

> ... Only Christ can get rid of the veil ... Whenever, though, they turn to face God as Moses did, God removes the veil and there they are—face-to-face! They suddenly recognize that God is a living, personal presence.
> 2 Cor. 3:15, 16 (MSG)

And the heart is softened.

> I will give you a new heart and put a new spirit in you; I will remove from you your heart of stone and give you a heart of flesh.   Ezekiel 36:26

As this person starts reading their Bible and applies it to their life, the seed of God's Word is planted in their hearts. As they yield to it, it begins to grow until it bears fruit. At this point, their heart is still soft towards God. But when they sin and do not keep close accounts with God; when God's Word is no longer treasured in their heart to keep them from sin, (Psalm 119:11) then sin creeps in and hardens the heart, eventually affecting their relationship with God. Through the deceitfulness of sin, a portion of your heart can become hardened again.

> But exhort one another daily, while it is called today; lest any of you be hardened through the deceitfulness of sin.   Hebrews 3:13 (KJV)

"Hardened" in the Strong's Concordance is the word "skleruno," and figuratively means, "to render stubborn."[2]

Sin hardens the heart and causes it to be stubborn. No wonder our prodigals have a difficult time accepting God's Word as truth. Not only does sin harden and cause one to have a stubborn heart, but it blinds as well.

> Speak to each other about these things every day while there is still time so that none of you will become hardened against God, being blinded by the glamour of sin.   Hebrews 3:13 (TLB)

> But whoever hates his brother is in the darkness and walks around in the darkness; he does not know where he is going, because the darkness has blinded him.   1 John 2:11

Sin hardens the heart, rendering it stubborn, and blinds us so that we cannot see clearly.

2Biblesoft's New Exhaustive Strong's Numbers and Concordance with Expanded Greek-Hebrew Dictionary. Copyright © 1994, Biblesoft and International Bible Translators, Inc.

To help you understand this truth, imagine that you are at a conference and the speaker has the salvation message clearly written out, point by point on a large poster board. You should be able to read it clearly and understand it because it is the Word of God, right? But part of the exercise is that you wear a veil over your eyes as you read it. The speaker walks up and down the aisle making sure that you can clearly see. But this veil takes the clarity away and you see dimly. In a similar way, this is what limits our prodigals from seeing clearly.

Did you get that? This truth in and of itself caused me to change the way that I minister to my loved ones. I am no longer prone to hitting them over the head with the Bible every time I see them. I don't know about you, but when I understood this truth, the light bulb went on and my heart was filled with compassion for them. I finally understood how important it is to bend my knee and pray for God to remove the blinders.

> '... Not by might nor by power, but by my Spirit,' says the LORD Almighty.
> Zechariah 4:6

You see, opening eyes is a supernatural work that only the Holy Spirit can accomplish. We must pray that God will remove the hardness of their hearts and enlighten their eyes and then share God's Word when He opens doors. Every decision that your prodigals make begins in their heart. This explains why your prodigal makes some bad decisions. The eyes of their spirit are not fully open. Pray the following prayer asking God to flood their eyes with light, floodlights that make everything visible.

Father, You can see everything. Flood their eyes with light!

> For I always pray to the God of our Lord Jesus Christ, the Father of glory, that He may grant you a spirit of wisdom and revelation [of insight into mysteries and secrets] in the [deep and intimate] knowledge of Him,

> By having the eyes of your heart flooded with light, so that you can know and understand the hope to which He has called you, and how rich is His glorious inheritance in the saints (His set-apart ones). Eph. 1:17-18 (AMP)

So we see that sin can blind and harden the heart. When the heart is hardened, it is unyielding just like hardened soil in a garden that has not been cultivated or watered and is filled with rocks and stones. It is difficult for seeds to take root in this type of soil. In the same way, a hardened heart can become resistant to the voice of God, to the seed of His Word.

Not only that, but when sin grows deep and takes a strong hold in our loved one's life, this gives Satan a place of influence in their lives. This sin, like a weed, can choke out the good seed of God's Word that has already been planted there. We see this in the Parable of the Seed and the Sower in Matthew 13:22 (AMP).

> As for what was sown among thorns, this is he who hears the Word, but the cares of the world and the pleasure and delight and glamour and deceitfulness of riches choke and suffocate the Word, and it yields no fruit.

SOWING SEEDS

*L*et's believe together for God to flood their hearts with light and dispel all darkness.

> And the Light shines on in the darkness, for the darkness has never overpowered it [put it out or absorbed it or appropriated it, and is unreceptive to it.].
> John 1:5 (AMP)

Do not underestimate God! When He floods their heart, they will begin to see! God works in amazing ways and He will get their attention. It might be in a dream, or through circumstances or by tugging at their heart and conscience. But He will get their attention and He will turn the light on when you pray!

At times, they will call you asking you to pray, and you will be able to respond by telling them that you have already been praying because God has forewarned you. (Isn't this exciting? That's how real God is!) The reality of who God is will become rooted in their heart and there will be no question of God's love and plans for their lives. At other times your wayward loved ones will seem closed and will not share with you, but you can be assured that God is at work and when you pray, He will shine the light of His Holy Spirit upon their hearts.

Prayer Journal:

Start journaling and praying on the following page. Ask God to do this daily.

Father, remove the veil that is blinding _____. (2 Cor. 3:16-17) For I always pray to the God of our Lord Jesus Christ, the Father of glory, that He may grant _____ a spirit of wisdom and revelation [of insight into mysteries and secrets] in the [deep and intimate] knowledge of Him, By having the eyes of her/his heart flooded with light, so that she/he can know and understand the hope to which He has called her/him, and how rich is His glorious inheritance in the saints (His set-apart ones), (Ephesians 1:17-18 AMP)

_____
_____
_____
_____
_____
_____
_____
_____
_____

Pray and Write !

Weeds & Tares

Weeds are one of the biggest nuisances to the gardener. Proverbs 22:8 in the Message Bible says whoever sows sin, reaps weeds. It seems as though weeds are always with us and can never be completely eliminated.

> Weeds and thorn bushes everywhere! Good for nothing except, perhaps, hunting rabbits. Cattle and sheep will forage as best they can in the fields of weeds—but there won't be a trace of all those fertile and well-tended gardens and fields. Isaiah 7:24-25 (MSG)

When weeds are loosened from the soil, they must be quickly removed. Weeds do not respect property lines and left unchecked, will rapidly spread, wrapping their roots around the good plants, strangling them.

> But while his men were sleeping, his enemy came and sowed tares also among the wheat, and went away. But when the wheat sprang up and bore grain, then the tares became evident also ... "Sir, did you not sow good seed in your field? How then does it have tares?" And he said to them, "An enemy has done this!" Matt. 13:25-28 (NASB)

A tare is a weed resembling wheat in appearance and size. But when it matures, its seed turns black and can be poisonous to humans and animals, causing sickness and death. Because it resembles wheat, it would be an easy way for the enemy to invade and plant seeds of destruction before anyone realized what was happening. Even so, when the enemy sows unsuspecting weeds of sin in your prodigal's heart, your loved ones can be deceived until the weeds of sin are full grown, raising their ugly black heads.

Your prayers can loosen weeds but your wayward loved ones must consent to the Holy Spirit as He removes them. That is why it is so important to aim your prayers toward their hearts. Your part is to pray and plant as the Holy Spirit leads. It is God's part to convict and, as your loved ones' eyes are opened and they surrender, the Lord will free them from the power of sin.

The Destructive Weed of Unbelief

... let us throw off everything that hinders and the sin that so easily
entangles ...   Hebrews 12:1

*B*ecause weeds have the capacity to produce thousands of seeds, they grow

quickly into strangling destroyers of faith.

One of the most destructive "seed weeds" in your heart is unbelief. It can squeeze the life out of promises planted in faith. Instead of producing a full crop, the good plants fall prey to the stealthy destroyers turning your heart garden into a playground for weeds.

The enemy sows a tiny weed seed of unbelief, and you can unwittingly help it grow with your words until your faith is weed-choked!

But while everyone was sleeping, his enemy came and sowed weeds
among the wheat, and went away.   Matthew 13:25

For example, you may be praying diligently for your wayward loved ones and in the next breath, while you are speaking with someone, you can negate your prayers by saying he will never come to the Lord. He is so stubborn!

Maybe this is one of the reasons why the promises you planted haven't bloomed? Perhaps you haven't given them enough time, or, could it be that there is a weed of unbelief strangling them? You must guard your heart from the weed of unbelief for it will rapidly choke the promises of God.

Therefore I say to you, all things for which you pray and ask, believe that
you have received them, and they shall be {granted} you. Mark 11:24
(NASB)

Do not underestimate God! Believe Him at His Word! Instead of speaking words of unbelief, speak God's promises into their lives.

Unbelief is not the only weed in the Garden of the Heart. Just as there are a multitude of different weeds in earthly gardens, so there are many types of weed sins that choke God's promises.

Ask boldly, believing without a second thought. People who "worry their prayers"
are like wind-whipped waves. Don't think you're going to get anything from the
Master that way, adrift at sea, keeping all your options open. James 1:6-8 (MSG)

Journal:

Father, show me if I have unbelief or any other sin that might be hindering my prayer life. Write about this in your journal.

MULCH

*E*ven as mulch is a protective covering over soil, PRAYER covers the heart

with protection from the enemy who wants to rob, kill, and destroy. Like mulch, prayer suppresses the weeds of sin, protecting you and your loved ones from the harsh winds of life, and safeguarding you from destruction.

As an intercessor it is vital that you guard your heart. For example if you find the sin of grumbling and complaining in your heart, confess it, turn from it and plant the seed of God's Word in its place through prayer like this.

Father, forgive me for complaining about this situation, I turn from it.

> In everything I will give thanks for this is the will of God in Christ Jesus concerning me. 1 Thessalonians 5:18

Praying like this stops sin from taking root. Diligently do so, because there are some sins that take such a strong hold in your heart as well as in your prodigal's.

A stronghold is a thought that raises itself against and above the will and the Word of God. Satan sows a suggestion and when received in areas of hearts that are not surrendered, it becomes their own.

Some perennial weeds have roots that grow as much as 25 feet into the ground. It is almost impossible to remove them. They wrap themselves around the good roots in plants and strangle the life out of them. They are very difficult to uproot. So it is with strongholds in our prodigals' hearts. Anger, bitterness, hate, alcoholism, drug addictions, pride, unbelief, pornography and other sins can have such a powerful hold on their lives that they spoil the good fruit that was planted earlier at salvation.

> ... Plow up the hardness of your hearts; otherwise the good seed will be wasted among the thorns. Jeremiah 4:3 (TLB)

For example, our ministry gets countless prayer requests for prodigals struggling with infidelity. I have heard of Christian men and woman who have been set free from lust, and have even preached about the detriments of lust and adultery. But over time, unsuspectingly, the enemy has snuck in, sowing seeds of lust and taking back territory. Before long this seed takes root and he/she is deceived, justifying sinful behavior. As the root of lust takes hold of their heart, they spend more time in fantasy (pornography, flirting, and cheating or online relationships), and less time in a healthy relationship with their spouse. The truth that they once believed has been choked out, their heart has hardened into deception, and they have grown comfortable with the sin in their life.

But thank God, He has not left us helpless. 2 Corinthians 10:4-5 says that He has given us divinely powerful weapons for the pulling down of these strongholds that are trying to choke out the good seed of God's Word from our prodigals' hearts.

Your prayers will cultivate their heart until they are softened and yielded to God again. Your prodigals cannot fight for themselves. **They need you to intercede for them. God expects you to cultivate their heart. Always remember, that:**

"... apart from me you can do nothing." Jesus said.   John 15:5

It is through the name of Jesus, that your prayers are empowered.

[Yes] I will grant [I Myself will do for you] whatever you ask in My Name
[as presenting all that I Am]...   John 14:13 (AMP)

SOWING SEEDS

*7*he Creeping Knapweed has roots that grow 25 feet into the ground and causes significant losses in croplands. Not only that, but it can produce 1200 more weed seeds that can remain dormant for five years! It has a pretty purple, white or pink flower that extends from its stem. By looking at it, you wouldn't think that it was so destructive. And once it is treated with herbicides, it must be monitored for five years to be sure that it is destroyed. Gardeners know that the best control for this weed is prevention.

In the same way, weeds in our wayward loved ones' hearts can take a strong hold. The best control is prevention. So let's pray proactively over their hearts, believing God to protect their hearts from sin taking a stronghold. And if any area of sin has already taken hold, your prayers can loosen it, making it easier for them to surrender to the Holy Spirit.

Let's take the sin of bitterness, for example. Its root system can grow extremely deep. Your wayward loved one might be holding on to all kinds of offenses. These thought systems, many times accusations of the enemy (Rev. 12:10), can grow deep into their hearts and take a strong hold in their heart.

Have you ever felt like you were making progress in their life when all of a sudden a misunderstanding occurs, the old weed of bitterness raises its ugly head and they are offended all over again? You wonder what just happened. It could be that the accuser of the brethren is taking the dormant seed and bringing it to the surface of their heart.

You are in a spiritual battle. Always remember you do not fight against flesh and blood.

> For we wrestle not against flesh and blood, but against principalities, against powers, against the rulers of the darkness of this world, against spiritual wickedness in high places. Ephesians 6:12 (KJV)

You must pray, pray, pray until these weeds are uprooted from their hearts. Go to the Seed Section and pray the Weed-Killer Scriptures.

Prayer Journal:

Father, Show me how to pray. Remove the sin of _____ from _____'s heart. I declare that the accuser of the brethren is powerless over his/her heart and over our relationship. Protect my heart from unbelief and resentment. I trust that You are at work in my loved ones' hearts. For You said in 1 John 5:14-15, "This is the confidence we have in approaching God; that if we ask anything according to His will, He hears us. And if we know that He hears us – whatever we ask -- we know that we have what we asked of Him."

Pray & Write...

Pulling Down Strongholds

> ... the weapons of our warfare are not carnal but mighty in God for pulling down strongholds, casting down arguments and every high thing that exalts itself against the knowledge of God, bringing every thought into captivity to the obedience of Christ.
> 2 Corinthians 10:4-5 (NKJ)

*T*he New American Standard (NASB) translation uses the word "fortresses" instead of "strongholds." These wrong-thinking patterns grow into a fortress protecting the mind from the truth. These fortresses keep God's Word out. When you pull down strongholds, these fortresses will be demolished. Reasoning with this person may not help.

When Satan or the world sows a thought that is contrary to God's Word into the mind, and a person receives it and accepts it as their own, it can take hold in their heart.

You can use the powerful weapons God has given you and uproot it through prayer. The Living Bible says,

> These weapons can break down every proud argument against God and every wall that can be built to keep men from finding him. With these weapons I can capture rebels and bring them back to God and change them into men whose hearts' desire is obedience to Christ.
> 2 Corinthians 10:5 (TLB)

> We use our powerful God-tools for smashing warped philosophies, tearing down barriers erected against the truth of God, fitting every loose thought and emotion and impulse into the structure of life shaped by Christ. Our tools are ready at hand for clearing the ground of every obstruction and building lives of obedience into maturity.
> 2 Corinthians 10:5-6 (MSG)

Michele was a prodigal who insisted that she did not believe in my God. Yet I knew that deep down she did because God had revealed Himself to her too many times for her not to believe. So for several weeks I prayed down this stronghold of unbelief. As I continued to intercede for her, the roots of unbelief that were strangling the truth of God's Word were finally loosened and she could see a glimmer of light. She called me for personal prayer and confessed that she must have some belief in her heart, as she was asking me for prayer.

As I prayed, this weed of unbelief loosened and God's light broke through until her spiritual eyes could see.

There are several ways that you will know what stronghold to pull down.

1. Listen to the Holy Spirit. He can reveal them to your heart, for He alone knows the hearts of all men. (1 Kings 8:39)

> But when He, the Spirit of truth, comes, He will guide you into all truth. He will not speak on His own; He will speak only what He hears, and He will tell you what is yet to come. He will bring glory to me by taking from what is mine and making it known to you. All that belongs to the Father is mine. That is why I said the Spirit will take from what is mine and make it known to you.   John 16:13-14

When I turned 40, wrinkles appeared on my face that really bothered me; more so than normal. I went to see my Pastor and shared my concerns. When he asked me to share an allegory of how I was feeling, from deep within my heart came these words; words that I had never thought about before. God was about to reveal a stronghold so that it could be removed.

I said, "When I was a little girl my mother was like a blanket around me. She gave me a sense of love, of worth and security. When she died, that blanket came off of me. I searched desperately for that blanket. In my 20s, I found something called beauty that felt just like her blanket. It gave me the same sense of love, worth and security. And now that blanket is coming off again and I don't know who I am."

God then spoke to my heart. He said, "I am your blanket. I am your love, your worth and your security."

I was set free. God exposed the root of the stronghold in my heart. I finally understood why aging was bothering me so deeply. I believed a lie; Satan knew my unmet need for love and deceived me into thinking that my outward appearance was who I was. It was such a subconscious thing that I was not even aware of it. I was looking to fill a void and the enemy filled it with a lie.

Like me, many times our prodigals do not know what strongholds are in their hearts or how they even got there. But God does and as you pray, God will do the work. Once your prodigal believes the lie, he or she might build a fortress of protection around it. This becomes a stronghold; a place from which the enemy can influence. Reasoning with them will not remove the stronghold. You must pray it down.

Continue to pray over their hearts. Remember, I prayed the heart scriptures over my own heart for many months and now God was deep at work fulfilling His Word, exposing the stronghold and healing me.

2. God has also given us a window into our prodigals' hearts. From the heart, the mouth speaks.

... For out of the overflow of his heart his mouth speaks ... Luke 6:45

Pay attention to what comes out of their mouth. Are they speaking words of fear, anger, hate, unbelief, pride or unforgiveness? Their words are a window into their heart. If you listen closely, the Lord will reveal what the strongholds are. Use listening as a tool, which aims deep into their heart. Once the weed is detected, your prayer will act just like a long narrow blade of a dandelion puller, uprooting the stronghold and allowing God's truth to grow in its place.

3. This is not a formula; it is co-laboring with the One who knows the hearts of all men.

> *... Lord, You know everyone's heart ...* Acts 1:24
>
> *... (For you alone know the hearts of men) ...* 2 Chronicles 6:30

In the back of this manual, within the Scripture Prayers you will find a prayer to help you pull down strongholds. Simply insert the person's name and the strongholds that God reveals to your heart. Pray daily until the person is set free.

It really is not complicated. As the Holy Spirit directs you, pick up this powerful weapon of prayer and pull down the stronghold. Each time you pull it down; it loosens its grip more until it is demolished. Then ask God to take their thoughts captive, conquer their rebelliousness and teach them to obey Christ. Do not be discouraged if you do not see immediate answers to your prayers. God is at work! For...

> *... Every plant which My heavenly Father did not plant shall be uprooted.*
> Matthew 15:13 (NASB)

SOWING SEEDS

*A*s the soil of the heart is cultivated, and strongholds are loosened, the seed of

God's Word will easily take root. Your prayers will prepare their hearts to receive the seed. When you pray from the category of heart scriptures in the back of this manual the Holy Spirit will soften the heart and bring to surface the hidden, hard things that have been buried for years, such as hurt or anger and false belief systems. As you pray down strongholds, He will break false theologies, pride and unbelief.

Prayer Journal:

Go there now on bended knee and continue praying until the soil of their heart is softened and receptive to the truth of God's Word. When planted, the truth of God's Word will change them. Revelation comes in seed form as the Holy Spirit drops a seed of the truth in their heart or a seed from the Word of God. Sometimes a stronghold is so deep that it might take a while to see results. But each time you pull, it loosens its grip more until it becomes easier for your prodigal to surrender to God.

Pray & Write...

Notes...

Seed Preparation

While the earth remains, seedtime and harvest…shall not cease.

Genesis 8:22 (NKJ)

Pray & Write...

Preparing the Seeds

The Seed of Life

*T*he seed of God's Word, **PLANTED** in the soil of the heart, will begin to swell and push everything out of its way; even as seed in an earthly garden pushes dirt, rocks, and weeds out of the way. It is powerful. But in order for it to grow in the heart, it must be planted. The Seed of God's Word is full of miracle-working power. When you look at a natural seed, you cannot see the power that is contained within. If the package says that the seed will produce a Sunflower, then you must believe it. In the same way, when you plant the seed of God's Word, you cannot see the end result immediately. **But underneath the soil of the heart, it is swelling, growing and eventually bursting open with new life; even though it may not be apparent for quite some time. So don't give up quickly! And don't miss this important principle**! You have to believe that the One who created it will bring the desired results. If you dig up the Sunflower to look at it every day, you will destroy it; it just will not produce. So it is in the spiritual garden. You must plant it and believe by faith. We must not underestimate God's miracle-working power.

According to Mark 4:14 (AMP), the Word of God is called the seed. Contained within each Scriptural seed is the embryonic life, or DNA, of the Living Word — Jesus Christ. When planted in the heart, the Divine Seed containing everything needed to bring forth life releases wonder-working power and transforms the soul into the image of Christ.

> … he has given us his very great and precious promises, so that through them you may participate in the divine nature and escape the corruption in the world caused by evil desires.   2 Peter 1:4

When you speak the Word of God, it actively carries out God's command, for the Word is **living** and **active,** and is full of creative life. (Heb. 4:12 NASB)

The Greek word for "**living**" is "**zao**," meaning "to live, to breathe; having vital power in itself and exerting the same upon the soul; to be full of vigor – to be fresh, strong, and efficient."

The Greek word for "**active**" is "**energes**," meaning "operative, effectual, and powerful."

The Word of God contains all the power to perform God's will because it contains the power within itself.

> So shall My word be which goes forth from MY mouth; it shall not return to me empty, without accomplishing what I desire, and without succeeding {in the matter} for which I sent it. Isaiah 55:11 (NASB)

The Word can be spoken in prayer over your loved one's heart, or as the Holy Spirit opens a door for you to speak directly to their heart. **Remember not to negate it by speaking destructive words of criticism, doubt and unbelief.** They will destroy the seed before it can sprout. When spoken in faith, the Word contains all the power needed to create life, just like it did at creation. Hebrews 1:3 tells us that Jesus holds all things together by the Word of His power. And that same power lives within you, because Jesus, the Living Word, lives within you. God is just waiting for you to speak and plant the Word so He can perform it.

> ... I am watching over My word to perform it. Jeremiah 1:12 (NASB)

> ... A farmer sowed his field and went away, and as the days went by, the seeds grew and grew without his help. For the soil made the seeds grow. First a leaf-blade pushed through, and later the wheat-heads formed and finally, the grain ripened. Mark 4:26-28 (TLB)

SOWING SEEDS

*D*id you know that garden manuals say some types of seeds can remain in the soil seed bank for more than 50 years before germination? No matter how long it takes, plant and keep planting. God's Word will not return void.

John prayed faithfully every day for the salvation of his friend, Doug. When John was on his deathbed, Doug still refused to come to the Lord. But when John was buried into the ground, Doug finally bent his knee and gave his heart to the Lord. John had planted God's Word into Doug's heart and believed for years. Yet he did not see the harvest during his time on the earth. But God's Word did not return void. At the right time God, the Master Gardener will cause the seed that was planted to sprout forth.

Prayer Journal:

Find a seed in the back of this journal under the categorized scriptures. Write it on your prodigal's page and begin planting it, through prayer, into the heart of your prodigal.

Seeding Process

*L*et's take a look at the process a seed goes through from germination to harvest, in order to fully understand how to plant the seed of God's Word into our prodigal's hearts.

Soak the Seed...

*M*ost gardeners know if they soak their seeds prior to planting, they will germinate or sprout faster. When seeds are prepared this way, they will have a greater success rate of germination after they're planted.

In the same way, when you get on your knees and soak in the presence of Christ through personal time with Him, allowing Him to permeate your very being, you create an ideal condition for your prayer seeds to spring up at an increased rate.

> For as the soil makes the sprout come up and a garden causes seeds to grow, so the Sovereign LORD will make righteousness and praise spring up before all nations.   Isaiah 61:11

Therefore, spend time worshipping God before you enter into your prayer time. Entering into the presence of God is not always easy. In fact, the psalmist wrote that he offered up to God the sacrifice of thanksgiving (Psalms 116:17), and the Apostle Paul encouraged us to offer up to God the sacrifice of praise (Heb. 13:15).

When you observe all that is occurring in your prodigal's circumstances, you might find it difficult to praise God – it feels like a sacrifice. You might not feel like praising God, but praise Him anyway, even when you feel discouraged. Doing so will usher in His presence, for He inhabits the praises of His people (Ps. 22:3 KJV).

SOWING SEEDS

*P*ractice praising Him until it becomes a way of life. Prayer is all about relationship, not performance. Praise is where God lives. (Psalms 22:3)

Here are a few biblical examples of victory through praise!

> 21After consulting the people, Jehoshaphat appointed men to sing to the LORD and to praise him for the splendor of his holiness as they went out at the head of the army, saying: "Give thanks to the LORD, for his love endures forever." 22As they began to sing and praise, the LORD set ambushes against the men of Ammon and Moab and Mount Seir who were invading Judah, and they were defeated.
>
> 2 Chronicles 20:21-22

> 25But about midnight, as Paul and Silas were praying and singing hymns of praise to God, and the [other] prisoners were listening to them, 26Suddenly there was a great earthquake, so that the very foundations of the prison were shaken; and at once all the doors were opened and everyone's shackles were unfastened.
>
> Acts 16:25-26 (AMP)

Prayer Journal:

You already have the victory! Jesus Christ won it for you at Calvary.

Father, thank You for Your victory and for working in the hearts of my loved ones. You are faithful! I trust that You Who began a good work in my loved ones will complete it to the day of Christ Jesus. (Phil 1:6) Lord, I praise you for forgiving all of my sins and cleansing me from all unrighteousness (1 John 1:9). I praise You, for nothing is too difficult for You (Jer. 32:17).

I praise You because You are the One who sustains me (Ps. 3:5; 18:35; 54:4). You are able to do immeasurably more than I could ever ask or imagine, according to the power that works within me (Eph. 3:20).

Spend time with God writing out a prayer of praise in your journal!

Plant the Seed...

$\mathcal{W}$hen it's time to plant, get down on your knees, dig deep into the soil and don't worry about getting dirty – the seed will grow into an abundant harvest. That's the fun of co-laboring with God! He's already promised the return on investment.

Even as the gardener plants his seed in the readied soil, you must plant in the heart by praying a Scripture promise, personalizing it with personal pronouns as you speak it out. God's Word is powerful, and even though God can do anything, He has chosen to work <u>with</u> us as His co-laborers. He gave us His Word to plant in the hearts of men and women.

> His divine power has given us everything we need for life and godliness through our knowledge of him who called us by his own glory and goodness. 2 Peter 1:3

Just because we are Christians, we cannot sit back, do nothing and expect God's Word to grow in the hearts of our wayward loved ones. He has given us His Word and as we plant it, He will bring growth. It is so important for you to know God's Word and to have it hidden in your heart so the Holy Spirit can bring it up to pray at the appropriate time. **Knowing God's Word is a powerful weapon against the enemy. We must read it, hide it in our hearts, live it and speak it out.**

For example, perhaps your prodigal is bound by fear. Find a related verse in the SEED portion of this journal under FEAR and, pray it this way.

"For God has not given _____ a spirit of fear, but of power and of love and of a sound mind." (2 Tim. 1:7 NKJV) _____ shall not fear anything except the Lord of the armies of heaven! If _____ fears him, she/he need fear nothing else." (Is. 8:13 TLB)

Or possibly you are struggling with the fear of what will happen to your loved one. You can pray this way.

I do not fear the terror that comes by night (Ps. 91:5), or have any fear of bad news. My heart is steadfast, trusting in You. My heart is secure and I have no fear (Ps. 112:7), because You are my hiding place. You will protect me from trouble and surround me with songs of deliverance (Ps. 32:7).

As you continue to proclaim the Word and believe it has already happened, though unseen, the power of God breaks forth and your wayward loved ones are set free.

Do you believe that God's Word contains His life? If you do, then what is holding you back? Start praying and proclaiming it! **Do not underestimate the power of His word. It brings forth new life!**

By praying God's Word, you take possession of it and hide it in your heart where it can sprout. As you continue to proclaim the Word and believe it has already happened, though unseen, the power of God goes forth bringing results.

> Therefore I say to you, all things for which you pray and ask, believe that you have received them, and they shall be {granted} you.   Mark 11:24 (NASB)

Label the Seed...

*O*nce a seed is planted, a gardener will often take a stick and label it with a picture and name of the plant to remind her of what's growing underground.

Follow this example and record each dated scripture request in your prayer journal. Write out the entire verse, or refer to it in the SEED section of your journal. This way you will consistently keep the promise of God before your eyes as you picture the answer in its fullness.

> But the word is very near you, in your mouth and in your heart, that you may observe it.   Deuteronomy 30:14 (NASB)

I love adding pictures to my prayer pages. It brings the reality of who I am praying for in a fresh and vibrant way. Looking at a picture of the person I am praying for causes me to slow down and connect my heart to who they really are, to who God created them to be. It helps me to sense the uniqueness of this person and God's love for them. Keeping a prayer journal has many benefits. It will:

1. Keep you on track in your prayer life.

2. Give evidence of what God is doing.

3. Encourage you to pray more as you see God's answers.

4. Leave a legacy of God's love for your loved ones. Just think how powerful it will be when your prodigal comes back to the Lord and you hand them the legacy of your prayer journal; the proof that God answers prayer. I don't know about you, but I think that this will be a very powerful witness of God's unfailing love in their lives.

5. Strengthen your faith.

6. Stir you to pray even more.

7. Help you to believe God for the impossible!

When a gardener plants a seed, he could easily forget what was planted. But labeling his seed is a reminder, especially before the plant sprouts. It helps him to believe by faith that something is growing beneath the surface of the ground. In the same way, labeling your seed by writing out your request will help you keep your eyes on God's promises and not on your loved ones' circumstances.

When people ask me how I can keep standing for my wayward loved ones, I respond, "Standing on God's Word is what keeps me standing when I am in the midst of a storm." As you stand on the Word, it will become more real to you than your loved ones' circumstances. Even though I might see nothing else, I know that God's Word says He will rescue the seed of the righteous!

Water the Seed...

*S*o you've cultivated the land of the heart, planted some seeds in your garden, and labeled them so you won't forget what you planted, now what? It's time to pray for the rain of the Holy Spirit by thanking Him for growth; even before it is visible.

By thanking God with expectant faith for what He is doing, your seed will be kept moist with the rain of the Holy Spirit. In order to germinate, a seed must be watered and kept moist. When watered, moisture will be absorbed through the seed coat of the embryo causing it to swell. It helps me to picture it swelling more and more each time I pray. Finally, the swelling will be so great that it will cause the seed coat to crack open with new life.

Through this illustration, you can see how important it is to water your seed. As you continue to believe and focus on the Word instead of your circumstances, God will pour out His Spirit and cause the embryonic life of Christ to break forth.

> Just as rain and snow descend from the skies and don't go back until they've watered the earth, doing their work of making things grow and blossom, producing seed for farmers and food for the hungry, so will the words that come out of my mouth not come back empty-handed. They'll do the work I sent them to do; they'll complete the assignment I gave them. Isaiah 55:10-11 (MSG)

You will find that as you speak the Word in faith, the seed will not only affect the spiritual realm of your prodigal's life, but it will take root in your heart and water **YOU** as well.

> The liberal person shall be enriched, and he who waters shall himself be watered. Proverbs 11:25 (AMP)

> [Remember] this: he who sows sparingly and grudgingly will also reap sparingly and grudgingly, and he who sows generously (that blessings may come to someone] will also reap generously and with blessings.

> Let each one [give] as he has made up his own mind and purposed in his heart, not reluctantly or sorrowfully or under compulsion, for God loves (He takes pleasure in, prizes above other things, and is unwilling to abandon or to do without) a cheerful (joyous, "prompt to do it") giver [whose heart is in his giving].
>
> And God is able to make all grace (every favor and earthly blessing) come to you in abundance, so that you may always and under all circumstances and whatever the need be self-sufficient [possessing enough to require no aid or support and furnished in abundance for every good work and charitable donation].
>
> As it is written, He [the benevolent person] scatters abroad; He gives to the poor; His deeds of justice and goodness and kindness and benevolence will go on and endure forever!
>
> And [God] Who provides seed for the sower and bread for eating will also provide and multiply your [resources for] sowing and increase the fruits of your righteousness [which manifests itself in active goodness, kindness, and charity].
> 2 Corinthians 9:6-10 (AMP)

So don't be surprised when the same scriptures you planted in your prodigal's heart wash over your own heart. God is always waiting to water us with His Word.

> ... And you shall be like a well watered garden and like a spring of water whose waters fail not.
> Isaiah 58:11 (AMP)

Begin thanking God for the promises of His Word. Don't just think about it. Call those things that are not as though they are, thanking God for what you do not see with your visible eyes and what He said He would do (Romans 4:17). Instead of negative talk, whining and complaining, speak the Word, which gives life. As you do, God will open up His water supply.

SOWING SEEDS

*I*t is now time to turn your asking into thanking. You have planted the seed.

Continue taking hold of the promises and believe that they will sprout forth. This is a vital part of the planting process. Thank God for the growth that is happening in the hearts of your loved ones.

> This is the confidence we have in approaching God: that if we ask anything according to his will, he hears us. And if we know that he hears us – whatever we ask – we know that we have what we asked of him. 1 John 5:14-15

When you pray God's Word, you are praying God's will and therefore, you can believe that He heard you and that He is at work in their lives!

Prayer Journal:

Go to your prayer pages and look at the scripture that you have written under the name of your prodigal. Thank God for His promise. Yes, thank Him even before the answer comes.

> ... He comes as rain comes, as spring rain refreshing the ground. Hosea 6:3 (MSG)

Pray like this:

Thank You Father, that the seed of the righteous shall be delivered, that the veil is removed from their eyes, that you have given them spiritual eyes that see, that Satan is a defeated foe in their life, that they are free from sin, from all bondages and death, and that salvation is theirs, in Jesus name, Amen.

Pray and Write!

Pray & Write...

Deepen the Roots

Rooted in Faith...

*H*ave you ever wondered what happens underground once the seed has been planted and watered? When a gardener waters his seeds, it swells until tiny root hairs protrude from the seed coat of the embryo. They absorb water and attach to particles of the soil. Roots then emerge from the embryo to provide the stability and nutrients needed for healthy growth. Amazing, isn't it? All of that is happening in a secret place underground!

When the seed of God's Word is planted in the secret place of the heart, it too begins to take root, becoming established in faith. Even though you may see nothing! As a gardener looks through eyes of faith and calls her seed by what it will become, so you must do the same thing by calling those things that don't yet exist as if they do – for you must live by faith, not by sight.

Rooted in Love ...

… May your roots go down deep into the soil of God's marvelous love.

Ephesians 3:17 (TLB)

*P*rayer is not the only element that will cause your prayer seed to take deep root within your prodigal's heart. Unconditional love from <u>YOU</u> and God is vital as well.

The Wild Rose Bush

My friend, Kathy, found out that I never had a rosebush in my garden so she gave me a wild rose bush. Upon handing it to me she said, "Take this bush home and plant it and water it daily. But whatever you do, don't pick any of the blooms this summer."

Once home I grabbed my shovel and dug a hole, carefully planting the wild rose bush. Faithfully, I watered it, but its promising pink buds withered and its green thorny stalks turned brown and brittle. The wild bush appeared to be doing its own thing – dying!

Every morning I looked for life, but found none. Kathy's words rang in my ears: "For the first year, don't try helping the plant by picking the blooms, even if they appear dead, or you'll bring about its demise."

I waited. The plant appeared dead and there was no visible sign of life. I contemplated whether I should uproot the unsightly plant.

A month later I took a stroll in my garden and noticed that the rose bush had sprouted new green stems and foliage as if they were grafted in. The wild bush wasn't dead after all!

Puzzled, I asked Kathy why the perishing bush suddenly came back to life. Her response surprised me.

"If you pick dead buds or stems when the bush is first planted, all the nutrients will be used to replace lost buds. But if you leave the dead buds alone, life will shoot downward supplying all it needs to root firmly in the soil. Unless properly rooted, it will wither and die."

So it is in the heart of the wayward. Once your prayer is planted, don't try fixing their wild, unruly ways by picking at apparent dead things in their life. If you do, they'll use all their strength bearing fruit in their own efforts instead of rooting deeply in Christ. The result will be a fruitless, man-pleasing person. With roots shallow and unstable, their spiritual life will dry up.

Don't determine growth only by outward appearances, look at the heart. Even though there may be no visible progress, you can be certain that God is working deep within their heart. When you start to see the signs of life coming from your wayward loved ones, don't try to help them along by picking at all the things that still need to change. Rather, continue to pray for them and love them. There is power in God's love reaching forth through your life that will open and melt the hardest of hearts.

Do you want to win them to Christ? Then love them unconditionally. But how do you do that when they have hurt you so badly? It's through the love of God, which has been shed abroad in your heart through the Holy Spirit (Romans 5:5).

All things in the Christian realm are released by faith. No matter what has happened in your relationships with your wayward loved ones, you <u>can</u> love them by faith. As you walk in love in obedience to God, He will meet you there, for God is love (1 John 4:16).

If you are patient and do not give up, you will soon see newness of life bursting forth. Remember, picking buds prematurely stunts growth.

*U*nconditional love is a key that will keep the door of your prodigals' hearts

open to you and to God who lives within you! If you use this key wisely, God's truth will easily be imparted into the hearts of your loved ones. Your prodigals must experience more than just your prayers and words. Unless they meet Christ's love through your life, you are a noisy gong. (1 Corinthians 13:1) And no one wants to listen to a noisy gong for very long without running away.

Are you having a difficult time loving them? Then remember that the love of God has been shed abroad in your heart, by the Holy Spirit Who lives within you. (Romans 5:5 KJV) Your faith will work according to the measure of love that you walk in. They go hand in hand, for faith works by love. (Gal. 5:6)

Prayer Journal:

Father, thank You for shedding Your love in my heart. I loose it in Jesus' Name. Flood my heart with love, <u>Your</u> love, for my loved ones. Help me to put our differences aside. Help me to show them acts of kindness. Give me wisdom to know how to love them.

Patience ...

*U*nseen beneath the soil, the embryonic stem starts to sprout upward as two

small seed leaves begin to reach toward the light. Because every seed germinates at a different rate, it's important for the gardener to be patient and not get discouraged when she can't see any outward sign of growth.

Know that the Master is working on your behalf before you can see the evidence of your prayer. That's why it is so important not to waver in unbelief, but fix your hope on the One who can bring it to pass. Don't be discouraged if someone has his or her prayer answered before you. God's ways are not your ways, so you may not always understand why, at times, it seems to take so long. While you hope for what you do not see, be patient as you eagerly wait for the answer.

> And let us not grow weary while doing good for in due season we shall reap if we do not lose heart.
> Gal. 6:9 (NKJ)

Perseverance ...

*H*old fast the word and bear fruit with perseverance. (Luke 8:14, 15)

Perseverance is the quality that doesn't yield to circumstances. If you desire to reap the fruit of your labors, you must be like the farmer who doesn't give up regardless of what the winds of adversity sweep in. He sets his hand to the plow, seeding, weeding and watering with much perseverance, knowing if he falls under the circumstances of life, his garden will deteriorate. Likewise, the life of your spiritual garden depends on you appropriating Christ's perseverance in order to overcome the circumstances of life; all the while pushing forward with your hand to the plow till you see the fruit of your labors.

> Let us not become weary in doing good, for at the proper time we will reap a harvest if we do not give up.   Galatians 6:9

> So do not throw away your confidence; it will be richly rewarded. You need to persevere so that when you have done the will of God, you will receive what he has promised.   Hebrews 10:35-36

Waiting ...

> ... but those that wait upon the LORD, they shall inherit the earth.
>   Psalm 37:9 (KJV)

I love the word "inherit" in this verse. In the Hebrew it means, "to take possession of, to possess, and to occupy." The word has a legal sense of invasion for the purpose of taking the territory and settling into it. **You CAN take territory through prayer as you stand on God's promises.**

After standing on the promises of God, are you waiting? Or have you given up? It is so easy to pray and then give up because we do not see the answer right away. If you are waiting in unbelief and hopelessness, then you are not waiting at all. You have given up.

Waiting is not a passive word. "Wait" in the Hebrew means to, "expect, to await, look for patiently, to hope, to be confident, to trust and to be enduring."

Let's take a look at Isaiah 40:31 (KJV)

> But they that wait upon the LORD shall renew their strength; they shall mount up with wings as eagles; they shall run, and not be weary; and they shall walk, and not faint.

Those who are waiting are not just sitting around doing nothing. They are moving forward, walking, running. They are **NOT** standing still. I like what the Parallel Bible says about this verse. It says that those who are awaiting the fulfillment of His promises shall renew their strength.

Are you waiting? Do not be passive. You must diligently lay hold of your inheritance through believing prayer. Once you pray, begin to thank God for what He is going to do. Begin to expect and look for the answer patiently, be confident, trust God and be enduring.

In the parable of the Prodigal Son (Luke 15:11-32), Scripture tells us that the father saw him returning, "while he was still a long way off." This means he was <u>actively</u> watching. He was constantly watching for his son's return.

> So he got up and came to his [own] father. But while he was still a long way off, his father saw him and was moved with pity and tenderness [for him]; and he ran and embraced him and kissed him [fervently].   Luke 15:20 (AMP)

> Wait for the Lord; Be strong, and let your heart take courage; Yes, wait for the Lord.   Psalm 27:14 (NASB)

> And therefore the Lord [earnestly] waits [expecting, looking, and longing] to be gracious to you; and therefore He lifts Himself up, that He may have mercy on you and show loving kindness to you. For the Lord is a God of justice. Blessed (happy, fortunate, to be envied) are all those who [earnestly] wait for Him, who expect and look and long for Him [for His victory, His favor, His love, His peace, His joy, and His matchless, unbroken companionship].   Isaiah 30:18 (AMP)

<u>You are the watchman on the wall for your wayward loved ones. Wait for the Lord to act on behalf of your loved ones. Watch and wait and trust God to do what He said He would do.</u> "Trust" in the Hebrew is, "a confident expectancy of what God is going to do." Not a constant anxiety. It is a knowing that the rug won't be pulled out from underneath you.

> Since ancient times no one has heard, no ear has perceived, no eye has seen any God besides you, who acts on behalf of those who wait for him.   Isaiah 64:4

SOWING SEEDS

Prayer Journal:

Stand on that promise right now for your loved ones.

Lord, I take my stance and I will watch and wait and trust You. I confidently expect You to move in the life of those whom I am praying for.

Today, practice waiting. Remember waiting is active.

> I wait for the LORD, my soul does wait, and in His word do I hope. My soul waits for the Lord More than the watchmen for the morning; indeed, more than the watchmen for the morning.   Psalm 130:5-6 (NASB)

You can wait patiently, for God loves His lost sheep and will go out to find them.

> 3Then Jesus told them this parable: 4"Suppose one of you has a hundred sheep and loses one of them. Does he not leave the ninety-nine in the open country and go after the lost sheep until he finds it? 5And when he finds it, he joyfully puts it on his shoulders 6and goes home. Then he calls his friends and neighbors together and says, 'Rejoice with me; I have found my lost sheep.' I tell you that in the same way there will be more rejoicing in heaven over one sinner who repents than over ninety-nine righteous persons who do not need to repent. Luke 15:3-7

Or take another illustration:

> "... A woman has ten valuable silver coins and loses one. Won't she light a lamp and look in every corner of the house and sweep every nook and cranny until she finds it? 9And then won't she call in her friends and neighbors to rejoice with her? 10In the same way there is joy in the presence of the angels of God when one sinner repents."   Luke 15:8-10 (TLB)

Your wayward loved ones are more precious than silver. Therefore light your prayer lamp, sweep the house and search carefully until you find that which is lost; whether it is salvation or that part of Christ's character that is not evident in their lives.

Pray & Write. . .

Notes...

Gardening Tools

… Our tools are ready at hand for clearing the ground of every obstruction and building lives of obedience into maturity.

2 Corinthians 10:6 (MSG)

Pray & Write. . .

Gardening Truths

Record the Growth

*E*ventually, two green specks will peek out from the soil and reach upward toward the sun. Once the seedling shows outward signs of growth, the gardener records the changes seen, and continues to keep the soil moist until the plant is strongly rooted.

Don't stop praying just because you see the first signs of change and spiritual growth, for your plant is very tender. Continue to keep the soil moistened in prayer so the roots grow down into Christ and draw up nourishment from Him. Make notations of outward growth in the REAPING section of your prayer journal. By recording these changes, your faith will be encouraged and you will see the progress made. As your plant – your Prodigal's heart – grows strong and vigorous in the truth, it becomes rooted and grounded in Christ unto the fruit-bearing stage.

> Write, therefore, what you have seen, what is now and what will take place later.
> Revelation 1:19

Recording the growth is a very important part of prayer. This will help you to see what God is doing in your loved one's life and it will encourage you to press on in prayer. There may be periods where you do not see much happening. Occasionally review your journal so that you do not forget what God has done.

This will also be a testament for your prodigal to read when she/he comes back to the Lord. It will help them to understand God's unfailing love for them, and help them to receive His forgiveness for past failures.

Look through eyes of faith and call those things that don't exist yet as if they do!

Pray & Write...

Working the Garden

Sowing and Reaping

> While the earth remains, seedtime and harvest...shall not cease.
>
> Genesis 8:22 (NKJ)

To "sow" means to plant a seed in order to increase its return. In other words, when you plant a seed in the ground, you can expect many more seeds to be multiplied just like it. Following this principle, God planted the Divine Seed in the human heart expecting it to reproduce and change hearts to the likeness of His Son.

> I tell you the truth, unless a kernel of wheat falls to the ground and dies, it remains only a single seed. But if it dies, it produces many seeds. John 12:24

What do you expect to harvest through your prayers? Are you planting seeds of love, or are you planting seeds of anger and bitterness into your prodigal's life?

> ... for whatever a man sows, this he will also reap.   Galatians 6:7 (NASB)

This is one of the laws of God's kingdom! Whatever you sow you will reap. Be careful, however, for this principle operates the same regardless of what you plant.

> If he sows to please his own wrong desires, he will be planting seeds of evil and he will surely reap a harvest of spiritual decay and death ... Galatians 6:8 (TLB)

> They sow the wind, and reap the whirlwind ...   Hosea 8:7 (NKJ)

With what measure will you reap?

> ... He who sows sparingly will also reap sparingly, and he who sows bountifully will also reap bountifully.   2 Corinthians 9:6 (NKJ)

> Those who sow in tears will reap with songs of joy. He who goes out weeping, carrying seed to sow, will return with songs of joy carrying sheaves with him.
>
> Psalm 126:5-6

Today begin to sow seeds of life into the heart of your prodigal. Be patient as you wait for God to answer your prayers. Hold fast the Word and bear fruit with perseverance.

> And let us not grow weary while doing good, for in due season we shall reap if we do not lose heart.   Galatians 6:9 (NKJ)

SOWING SEEDS

$\mathcal{D}$o not give up no matter how long it takes. Set your hand to the plow, seeding, weeding, and watering with much perseverance and God will give the increase.

Aim for the heart! It is the door to your loved one's return!

> The seed will grow well, the vine will yield its fruit, the ground will produce its crops, and the heavens will drop their dew. I will give all these things as an inheritance to the remnant of this people.   Zechariah 8:12

> When you go through deep waters and great trouble, I will be with you. When you go through rivers of difficulty, you will not drown ...   Isaiah 43:2 (TLB)

Are the floodwaters of life keeping you from planting seeds of faith? Do you feel overwhelmed by insurmountable obstacles? If so, do not be discouraged or fearful, but continue to sow your seed for even in the midst of adversity it will take root and produce a harvest.

> Happy and fortunate are you who cast your seed upon all waters [when the rivers overflow its banks; for the seed will sink into the mud and when the waters subside, the plant will spring up; you will find it after many days and reap an abundant harvest] ...   Isaiah 32:20 (AMP)

Prayer Journal:

Sometimes the heart softens and changes almost immediately. At other times I have found that there is a fight of faith that needs to be fought. Press in and pray until the change comes. Spend time in prayer today, practicing everything that you have learned.

> Come, let us worship and bow down, Let us kneel before the LORD our Maker.
> Psalm 95:6 (NASB)

The Neglected Garden

*A*ny gardener intimate with the soil will tell you it takes intense work to keep it pliable, make it fertile, and keep the weeds and bugs at bay after seeds are planted. Even as diligence and wisdom are necessary to safeguard the earthly garden from harmful intruders, so it is with the heart. You must diligently claim the promises of God to shield your garden from all that would harm it. For then your heart will once again burst forth into bloom, filling the entire world with fruit. (Isa. 27:6, Isa. 35).

> I went by the field of the lazy man,
> And by the vineyard of the man devoid of understanding;
> And there it was, all overgrown with thorns;
> Its surface was covered with nettles
> Its stone wall was broken down.
> When I saw it, I considered it well;
> I looked on it and received instruction:
> A little sleep, a little slumber,
> A little folding of the hands to rest;
> So shall your poverty come like a prowler,
> And your need like an armed man.　　　Proverbs 24:30-34 (NKJ)

The stone wall was broken down and every predator was welcome to come into this unkempt garden to strip it of its fruit. Neglect had taken its toll. Spreading tendrils of strangling weeds suffocated the life out of any remaining plants. What was once a flourishing site of beauty, heavy laden with fruit and flowers, was now an infested wasteland covered with briars and thorns. What happened?

Even though God's wall of protection around us cannot be broken down, the heart can remove itself from God's protection and walk outside of His unmovable walls of grace, where it is susceptible to all manner of attack. With neglect, the heart's garden deteriorates just as an earthly garden does.

As the ground became hard and compacted from insufficient cultivation and watering, the once delightful garden had now become a playground for weeds.

In Proverbs 24, Solomon observed the consequences of laziness and ignorance and received instruction. Let's be wise and learn from the mistakes of others. We are called to be a watchman on the walls of our loved ones' hearts. They are the ones who will be held responsible for their own choices and sin.

While we may not be responsible for their sin, we will be held accountable for our prayerlessness. I know this is a sobering thought, so with it, let me remind you that prayer is all about relationship with God, and not praying just to get our prayers in!

You don't have to struggle to pray, just engage with the Master Gardener in prayer any time of the day.

> As for me, far be it from me that I should sin against the LORD by failing to pray for you …   1 Sam. 12:23

> I have set watchmen upon your walls, O Jerusalem, who will never hold their peace day or night, you who (are His servants and by your prayer) put the Lord in remembrance (of his promises), keep not silent.   Isaiah 62:6 (AMP)

You don't HAVE to spend time with God; you GET to spend time with God!

SOWING SEEDS

*S*olomon considered it well and received instruction. Will you? Even if you have been neglectful you can begin right now. It is not too late!

Don't beat yourself up for your lack of prayer. We all struggle with prayer from time to time.

Prayer Journal:

Go back to page 16 and re-read your commitment to pray and recommit all over again. If you are recommitting, add another date to your committal page.

When my children were little, I struggled with condemnation over my lack of prayer. One morning, heaviness fell upon me. I felt like such a failure. I stood at my kitchen counter and cried out to God,

> "Lord I am such a failure. Please forgive me. I am not praying enough or reading my Bible. Please forgive me."

This heaviness stayed with me throughout the day. That night I tucked my children in bed. I crawled into my bed and cried out once more,

> "God I am so sorry, I am such a failure."

Then I drifted off to sleep. In the middle of the night my 4-year-old daughter awakened me. I took care of her needs and then went back to bed. Once again I cried out to God,

> "Lord I will try harder. I am so sorry for failing you."

I finally fell back to sleep and a short time later my son woke me. So I slipped out of bed and took care of him. I went back to bed and cried out to God again until I fell fast asleep. The next time that I awakened, before I could even think, a scripture was floating through my mind.

> Who then will condemn us? Will Christ Jesus? No, for he is the one who died for us and was raised to life for us and is sitting at the place of highest honor next to God, pleading for us.   Romans 8:34 (NLT)

God was telling me that He was not condemning me. He loved me and died for me. This realization set me free. I no longer struggle with condemnation.

If you are struggling with condemnation and can't seem to get free, know that God does not condemn you; He loves you and wants to set you free. Surrender to Him and receive His forgiveness.

Father, forgive me for my failures. Thank you for not condemning me. I receive your help and grace In Jesus Name.

Take your place today as a co-laborer in the Garden of the Heart.

Years ago, I cried out to the Lord and said, "Lord make me a worshipper and an intercessor." He responded, "You already are a worshipper and an intercessor; now walk in who you are. I have made you a priest of God and a priest of God is a worshipper and an intercessor." (Rev. 1:6) and He has made us {to be} a kingdom, priest to His God and Father… (NASB)

> Seek the Lord and His strength; yearn for and seek His face and to be in His presence continually!   1 Chronicles 16:11 (AMP)

Prayer Journal:

Seek His face! He said, "Call on Me and I will show you great and mighty things that you do not know." God is inviting you to be a co-laborer in His garden. Write what you sense God speaking to your heart.

_____
_____
_____
_____
_____
_____
_____
_____Pray and Write !_____
_____
_____

Pray & Write....

Guarding Your Garden

Unseen Realms of Prayer

$\mathcal{A}$dam was called to be a keeper of the garden. This included guarding it and watching over it from dangerous elements and serpents. As you intercede for your prodigals, you must remain watchful. As you guard over their hearts, at times God will direct your prayers, warning you when danger is near. As you speak His Word, He will send forth His angelic troops, who perform and obey the voice of His Word, to battle against the evil forces of darkness on your behalf.

Someone's Watching

$\mathcal{M}$y mouth gaped open as the tall strange man approached my daughter, Katie. I was unprepared for what was to take place. Or was I?

For the last several mornings, the Lord instructed me to read Psalm 103.

> Bless the LORD, you His angels, Mighty in strength, who perform His word, obeying the voice of His word! Psalm 103:20 (NASB)

"Pray scripture promises of protection around your family. It will set My angels to work on your behalf," the Master spoke to my heart.

Without questioning, I prayed for my family's protection as He instructed, and I wrote it down in my journal.

The following evening Katie and I jumped into my Toyota and headed for Wal-Mart to shop for some school supplies.

Entering the parking lot, we saw a black Cadillac heading our way for the exit. The driver was a distinguished looking man in his fifties, and normally I wouldn't give him a second thought, but his icy stare unnerved me and sent chills up my spine. Averting my eyes from his, I clenched the steering wheel and proceeded to park in the near-empty lot. When Katie and I got out of the car, I saw his vehicle turn around, head back in our direction, and drive directly in front of our car.

As we quickly walked to the store entrance, I felt his eyes feasting on us like a vulture eyeing its prey. "Is he stalking us?" I wondered.

Thoughts of this creepy stranger wouldn't leave my mind, so about 20 minutes later, after checking out our purchases, I visually scouted the parking lot looking for him before we left the store. He wasn't anywhere in sight. Seeing an empty car parked next to mine, I breathed a sigh of relief, wrapped my arm around my pretty 11-year-old, and headed for our car. Then out of the blue he appeared, jumping out from between two cars ... coming straight at us!

His dark squinty eyes felt like piercing daggers as he made great-determined strides. My veins rushed with adrenaline. Trying to avoid his glaring evil eyes, I looked downward, and he walked right past us. But, unknown to me, he turned around and came up from behind us.

When Katie and I took a few more steps to get to the car, I removed my arm from her shoulder and proceeded to the driver's side while she went to the passenger's. You can imagine my horror as I saw him alongside her, standing within arm's reach. Then I realized it was his car parked next to ours!

What should I do? If I get in to unlock her door, he'll snatch her and throw her into his car. My mind froze.

Katie's bewildered eyes spoke volumes as she held the handle of the locked door waiting for me to do something. In seconds that seemed like hours I watched him rub his chin and repeatedly glance towards the front of the store, and then back towards Katie again. He seemed to be contemplating something. What was he doing? What should I do?

Think! Think!

Then I heard the inner Voice, "Get into the car and open her door."

Now, with a clear mind I hurriedly jumped in and unlocked her door. Immediately she climbed in and locked it again.

Safely inside with our hearts still pounding wildly, we watched the dazed-looking stranger staring in disbelief as his prey slipped through his fingers. Finally he slid into his car. We all just sat motionless for a few moments — the would-be abductor disappointed that the hunt was over, and us ... relieved.

Slowly backing out of the parking space, we headed for home, constantly looking over our shoulder to make sure he wasn't following. Finally safe and sound inside the house, Katie asked, "Mom, did you see that other man a few spaces down ... standing in front of a truck just staring at him?"

"No honey, I didn't ... are you sure?"

"Yes, I'm positive. I was afraid they were together."

"I didn't see anyone else." Then as if a light went on, "That must be why he hesitated and kept looking back and forth. He knew someone was watching him." As the enormity of the idea sank in, I fell into a chair and exclaimed, "Wow!"

Pulling out my prayer journal, I shared with Katie how the Lord had instructed me to pray earlier. All we could do was praise Him for His awesome answer to my prayers.

Was it an angel disguised as a man in front of that truck? I can only believe that it was because the Lord warned me for two days to pray His Word for angelic protection. As I did, His angels were released to work on our behalf as they obeyed the voice of His Word. By divine intervention, Katie and I were delivered from evil. God's intervention is cemented in her heart for eternity.

As you pray God's Word, it sets his angels to work on your loved one's behalf as well. Be sensitive to the Holy Spirit and pray as He directs you. Hearing God is one of the most important parts of effective prayer.

SOWING SEEDS

> Bless the LORD, you His angels, Mighty in strength, who perform His word, obeying the voice of His word!
> Psalm 103:20 (NASB)

*G*od's angels are ministering Spirits who are sent to protect you and minister to you and your loved ones. At times you might entertain them unaware. (Hebrews 13:2)

When you pray the Word of God, His angels will perform it on your behalf. When you speak out God's Word, it is like putting the sword of the spirit in your angel's hands! They stand ready for battle.

They hearken to the Word of God. They even came for Daniel's words.

> [11]And [the angel] said to me, O Daniel, you greatly beloved man, understand the words that I speak to you and stand upright, for to you I am now sent. And while he was saying this word to me, I stood up trembling. [12]Then he said to me, Fear not, Daniel, for from the first day that you set your mind and heart to understand and to humble yourself before your God, your words were heard, and I have come as a consequence of [and in response to] your words. [13]But the prince of the kingdom of Persia withstood me for twenty-one days. Then Michael, one of the chief [of the celestial] princes, came to help me, for I remained there with the kings of Persia.
> Daniel 10:11-13 (AMP)

When Daniel prayed, the angel told him that his prayer was answered 21 days prior! God did not withhold His answer – demonic forces delayed His angels. The angels were delivering the answer but the devil was fighting against it. When Daniel prayed, the battle was won in the heavenlies, before it was manifested on the earth.

Don't give up if you do not see results right away. Persevere until the answer comes to pass in this physical world. And remember, your angels are moving in response to your words. So don't hold back, speak out those promises!

Prayer Journal:

By now you should have scriptures under your prodigal's page and you should be praying Gods Word. Spend time there. Speak out God's promises and know that someone is waiting to come to your aid!

> ... He will give His angels [especial] charge over_____ to accompany and defend and preserve her/him in all your ways [of obedience and service]. Ps. 91:11 (AMP) Your angels, O Lord, encamp around ____and rescue_____ because she/he fears You.   Psalm 34:7

Listening

*W*hen we focus on Jesus He will alert us if darkness is approaching.

If you are watchful in prayer, the Holy Spirit may often alert you before you ever have concrete evidence that danger is near. He may do so through His still small voice, a word of knowledge, a discerning of spirits, dreams, visions, impressions or a burden. God speaks to each one of us differently.

> But when he, the Spirit of truth, comes, he will guide you into all truth. He will not speak on his own; he will speak only what he hears, and he will tell you what is yet to come.   John 16:13

God is always speaking to you, but are you listening? The ability to hear from God is vital if you are to follow Him. He can speak to you in a variety of ways ... through prayer, His Word, other people, our circumstances, by the Holy Spirit, and through dreams and visions. Through these avenues He'll warn, encourage, admonish, direct and give us wisdom.

Through obedience and regular fellowship with the Lord your spiritual hearing will be heightened until His voice is distinguishable from all others. The major key to knowing His voice is developing an intimate relationship with Him. There is no substitute!

Your number one priority in tending your garden is to keep yourself in a position to hear from God. He wants to lead you and guide you.

Below are several things you can do to keep yourself in a position to hear from God. I cannot stress enough how important it is that you position yourself to hear Him.

You must be born again

The most important requirement is to know Him personally, because Jesus said,

> My sheep hear my voice, and I know them, and they follow me.
> John 10:27 (KJV)

If you do not know Him personally, then today is the day of your salvation! He desires you to know Him intimately. Jesus Christ died for your sin, rose again and is seated at the right hand of the Father. If you believe that, confess your sin to Him and ask Him to come into your life, you will be saved. (Pray the prayer on p. 201-202)

Obedience

Intimacy begins and grows through your obedience, especially in the "small" things. You must obey the Lord's leading in order to hear from Him directly.

> The person who has My commandments and keeps them is the one who really loves Me; and whoever really loves Me will be loved by My Father, and I, too, will love him and will show, reveal, manifest Myself to him. I will let Myself be clearly seen by him and make Myself real to Him.
> John 14:21 (AMP)

Clean heart

Anything blocking your view of God – sin, unforgiveness, unbelief – will hinder your efforts for your Prodigal as well. The first order of business is to get yourself right with God and then focus on your prodigal. If you regard iniquity in your heart, He will not hear you. (Psalm 66:18)

> But your iniquities have made a separation between you and your God, and your sins have hidden His face from you, so that He will not hear. Isaiah 59:2 (AMP)

> Your iniquities have turned these blessings away and your sins have kept good [harvest] from you.
> Jeremiah 5:25 (AMP)

Sin blocks our communication with God; therefore it is important to keep your heart clean so that you can remain on praying ground.

Read God's word

The more you fill your heart with God's Word and meditate on it, the more sensitive you will become to God's voice.

> "Consider carefully what you hear," he continued. "With the measure you use, it will be measured to you – and even more. Whoever has will be given more; whoever does not have, even what he has will be taken from him." Mark 4:24-25

Worship

God gave you a heart to worship Him so you could commune directly with Him – don't squander that gift by failing to worship the only One worthy of our worship.

> ... God doesn't listen to evil men, but he has open ears to those who worship him and do his will.   John 9:31 (TLB)

Do not grieve the Holy Spirit

> And do not grieve the Holy Spirit of God, with whom you were sealed for the day of redemption.   Ephesians 4:30

The Holy Spirit is the One who leads you, guides you, counsels you, and warns you. The word, "grieve" in the Greek means, "to sadden, to cause grief, to offend." When we sin, we sadden the Holy Spirit. Our sin causes Him pain. The following verse describes some of the sins that grieve the Holy Spirit.

> Get rid of all bitterness, rage and anger, brawling and slander, along with every form of malice.   Ephesians 4:31

Heavenly Father, forgive me for grieving the Holy Spirit. Reveal my sin to my heart so I can confess it. Thank you for your forgiveness, In Jesus name, Amen.

SOWING SEEDS

*Y*ou cannot pray on your own. In spiritual battles you are powerless without God. Satan is not afraid of you, but of God in you. Therefore be careful not to grieve the Holy Spirit. He can warn you even before there is any evidence that danger is near.

Are you experiencing the fullness of God's Spirit or has the well of living water seemingly dried up?

The plowman could not till the parched, dry cracked earth due to the lack of rain. The people were experiencing drought. They were mourning. They were looking for water but the wells were dry. They were crying out to God, but God was not answering them. Why? Because they loved to wander from God's path. (Jeremiah 14 NASB)

If this is you, there is hope. Come to Him right now. He desires to flood your heart with springs of living water. God wants to empower you with His Holy Spirit. Jesus said that you would receive power after the Holy Ghost is come upon you. (Acts 1:8)

To be baptized means to be totally immersed, totally saturated with the Holy Ghost.

> You prepare a table before me in the presence of my enemies. You anoint my head with oil; my cup overflows. Psalm 23:5

> ... you have an anointing from the Holy One ... 1 John 2:20 (NASB)

Anointing means the smearing or rubbing of oil or perfume upon an individual. As you spend time with the Lord, He will press the Holy Spirit's power and anointing deeper and deeper into you. Allow Him to saturate you with the presence of His Spirit.

From His innermost being shall flow rivers of living water. (John 7:38) Innermost being in the word "koilia" means "womb." Did you know that you are God's womb on the earth? His womb of intercession. It is here, in your spirit where you labor and travail in prayer until Christ is formed in others. As you do, the Holy Spirit will birth His life into your prodigals.

Prayer Journal:

Use this journaling prompt to start a prayer dialogue with God.

Lord, fill me afresh with the power and the presence of Your Holy Spirit. I need You! I need...

_____
_____
_____
_____
_____
_____
_____
_____
_____

Pray and Write !

How God Speaks

*G*od may speak to us in a spectacular way, but usually He speaks to us in, "His still, small voice" in order to draw us near to Him in an intimate relationship.

> I will instruct you and teach you in the way which you should go; I will counsel you with My eye upon you.   Psalm 32:8 (NASB)

There may be a scripture floating through your mind, a thought impressed upon your mind, or someone's name coming to your heart. Or you may sense conviction in your conscience. This is God speaking to you.

At other times He might speak to you through the written Word & Rhema (the spoken word).

> ... the sword of the Spirit, which is the word of God.   Ephesians 6:17

The Greek word used in this verse is "Rhema." The Vine's Dictionary says that "Rhema" is an individual scripture, which the Holy Spirit brings to our remembrance for use in time of need. This may come through His still, small voice or through Scripture. The Holy Spirit illuminates the word, opening your eyes to understand it's meaning so that it is applicable to you today, in the circumstance in which you find yourself. When God gives you Rhema, it comes filled with His power just waiting to be released.

God might speak to you through circumstances, like when He opened and closed doors for Paul and Silas. They sensed a stop in their Spirit and said the Holy Spirit forbade them to go into some areas (Acts 16:6-9). Do not seek God's will through open and closed doors alone, however. Seek Him and He will reveal His plan to you however He desires. If you try to get direction from your circumstances apart from your relationship with God, they will not make sense.

Many times God speaks through words that people speak to you, but they must confirm what God is already speaking to your heart. If someone says that they have a word from the Lord for you, it should <u>always</u> confirm what the Lord has already spoken to your heart, or it may confirm what He will be speaking to you in the future.

Prayer Burdens

*Y*ears ago, my heart was burdened heavily for one of my children. I awoke with it, it remained with me all day, I went to sleep with it on my heart, when I woke in the night, the first thing on my heart was this child. This lasted for several months. Finally God broke through and gave me a word from the book of Isaiah telling me the battle was over. Peace filled my heart and God birthed in her heart what He was trying to do.

This is not a time of begging God but of praying in faith with all types of prayer as the Holy Spirit leads you. It is praying His promises, praying in the Spirit, praying with thanksgiving and praise even before it comes to pass in the natural.

A burden is heaviness or an apprehension in your spirit; it is a nudging to pray even though you may know nothing about the situation. When you sense God speaking to you in this manner, go at once and pray to see if He is calling you. Ask Him to remove it if it's not from Him, and then ask Him to increase it if it is from Him; so you can join the Holy Spirit in intercession according to His will.

> In the same way, the Spirit helps us in our weakness. We do not know what we ought to pray for, but the Spirit himself intercedes for us with groans that words cannot express. And he who searches our hearts knows the mind of the Spirit, because the Spirit intercedes for the saints in accordance with God's will.
> Romans 8:26-27

Apostle Paul understood this – he labored (travailed) through prayers and preaching until Christ was completely formed (molded) in people. (Gal. 4:19 AMP)

The Hebrew word for "travail" means, "To give birth or to bring forth." Travailing intercession might include strong physical manifestations in your prayer time, but it doesn't have to.

When we travail in prayer until Christ is formed in others, the Holy Spirit births His life into their hearts. The battle is raging in the heavenlies for the hearts of your wayward loved ones. Will you join the Lord in prayer for their souls?

Travailing in the Spirit does not have to be only with a deep groaning. At times it is ongoing intercession as the Holy Spirit births something through your prayers.

At times He speaks to us through peace or unrest in our spirit.

> Let the peace of God rule in your hearts ...   Colossians 3:15

The Amplified Bible says to let peace "act as an umpire." The peace of God will GUARD your heart and mind in Christ Jesus (Philippians 4:7). God's peace will literally act like an umpire to reveal God's will. If you have unrest about something, God is warning you. Wait until you have God's peace.

The closer you are to Him the more sensitive you'll become to His voice.

Whichever way God chooses to speak to you, it's important to record these things under your personal prayer page in your journal. By making this a habit, you'll have a record of how, when, and what God reveals to you. When you read your journal entries months (or even years) from now, you'll see the progress you've made, the obstacles you've overcome, and the areas that still need work. While learning to hear His voice, sift those revelations with the Word of God for accuracy, for He will <u>never</u> contradict His Word.

SOWING SEEDS

A few years ago one of my daughters called at 4:00 AM. She said, "Mom, can you pray for me? The last few nights everytime I try to go to sleep I feel this uneasiness." I said, "Yes, I will pray, but God has already gone before you. For the last few days, I, too, have been feeling an uneasiness when I tried to sleep, and I have already been prayng for you!" God goes before us.

Listen closely for the voice of the Holy Spirit and do not brush off His warnings. When God gives you a burden, the time to pray is NOW! You are an intercessor and you must stand in the gap and seek God's presence and intercede on behalf of others, enforcing the enemy's defeat. Do not brush off God's call. Someone's life may be depending on your prayers!

Keep your heart right before God. If your heart is filled with uneasieness due to sin, how will you be able to discern if God is giving you a prayer burden or if the heaviness you feel is due to sin or Satan's condemnation? One of your greatest defenses against the devil is to maintain a clean heart before God. Read His Word, seek Him and keep your heart clean like never before! God wants to move through your prayers!

Prayer Journal:

Time to get out your own Journal and commune with God – write down what He impresses on your heart. Trust me, you'll want a record to look back on in the weeks, months and years to come.

Knowing

*H*ow do you know if what you hear is from God? It isn't always easy, so you should listen carefully and test it within the context of Scripture.

When a voice isn't from Him you might experience confusion, fear or condemnation. You might have a check or uneasiness in your spirit. Pay attention to it, for the Lord is giving you a warning.

As you remain in communion with Him, He might speak intuitively to you, revealing something without anyone saying a word. This inward knowing never contradicts God's Word. It's the Holy Spirit confirming (bearing witness) with your spirit to guide you.

SOWING SEEDS

*H*ow often are you hearing from God? If you are not hearing Him regularly check your heart. God is not holding back. We take ourselves out of position to hear His voice. The more time you spend with Him, the more familiar you will be to His voice.

Prayer Journal:

Go to your journal and talk to God about this.

_____

_____

_____

_____

_____

_____

_____

_____

Pray and Write !

_____

Journaling

*W*hen it comes to hearing God's voice, journaling is invaluable because it slows you down long enough to hear from Him, and it invites Him to respond.

> I will stand on my guard post and station myself on the rampart; and I will keep watch to see what He will speak to me, and how I may reply when I am reproved. Then the LORD answered me and said, "Record the vision and inscribe {it} on tablets ..."
> Habakkuk 2:1-2 (NASB)

Journaling has been one of the greatest tools that God has used in my life to fine-tune me hearing His voice. When praying for your wayward loved ones, journaling becomes a tool to unload your struggles before God. Having a prodigal in your life can lead to:

- Disappointment
- Grief
- Fear
- Anger
- Confusion
- Depression
- Tears
- Broken relationships
- Judgment

If not dealt with, these feelings can paralyze you. Some people stop praying because it is all too difficult. **But now isn't the time to stop praying!** Your wayward loved ones need you now more than ever. You do not have to carry these concerns alone. God loves your prodigal more than you do. Use your journal to:

UNLOAD YOUR HEART: When you feel discouraged, write out your feelings to God and leave your burdens at the cross. This will help you to find His battle plan on how to pray for your loved ones. He will encourage you, strengthen you and impart His love into your heart for them. Be careful not to write about things too personal at the risk of others reading it. Alternatively, be sure to blacken out specifics with a marker.

WASH YOUR HEART: Remember, in order to pray effectively you must first keep your heart in a place where you can hear God. God's Word has a cleansing effect and will wash away the feelings that are not from Him. (Eph. 5:26)

RECORD GOD'S MOVEMENTS: Record what God is doing in your wayward loved one's life. This will encourage you to press on in prayer. It is easy to miss what God is doing if we are not looking closely. He is always at work and if we do not record His movements, it will be easy to forget.

LEAVE A LEGACY: When your prodigal finally comes back to the Lord, it will be so exciting for them to see how committed you were to pray for them. Once they realize what God has done, they will be drawn to Him even more deeply. They, too, will want to pray for others.

CREATE A BATTLE PLAN: Journaling is a great place to start creating your battle plan. Write what God shows you. This is important because you can easily lose your focus when circumstances get difficult. Writing it down will help you to keep your eyes on God and not on their circumstances. This will help you to keep your goal before your eyes.

> For the vision is yet for an appointed time, but at the end it shall speak, and not lie: thought it tarry, wait for it; because it will surely come, it will not tarry.
>
> Habakkuk 2:3 (KJV)

God will help you to develop a strategy. Spend time with Him daily and write down the battle plan that He gives you. As you assess the land of their heart, listen for:

- Obstacles hindering your prayers
- Scriptural directives
- Insight into their heart
- Revelation of strongholds
- Instructions on how to approach them
- Insights on how to love
- God's call to wait
- Forewarning of enemies' plans

Listen closely! For He goes before you! You will get the best results as you follow His plan. Record what He shows you and pray it through.

SOWING SEEDS

*J*ournaling will help you to keep short accounts with God. As an intercessor, hearing God is your lifeline. Apostle Paul kept his conscience clean before God and men. (Acts 24:16) He knew that in order for God to work through him, He would need to hear Him clearly. It is important to keep your heart clean so you remain on praying ground. When God convicts you of sin, don't brush it off. Stop, ask God to forgive you and turn from your sin. For... they will be delivered through the cleanness of your hands. (Job 22:30)

Prayer Journal:

Write for 10 minutes to God about the condition of your heart. Record His response. If nothing comes to you, then just wait in His presence without saying a word. Listen for His voice.

_____
_____
_____
_____
_____
_____
_____
_____
_____
_____
_____
_____
_____
_____
_____
_____
_____
_____
_____
_____
_____
_____
_____
_____
_____
_____
_____
_____
_____
_____
_____
_____
_____
_____
_____

Pray and Write!

Dreams

*I*n the last days God says,

> ... I will pour out my Spirit on all people. Your sons and daughters will prophesy, your young men will see visions, your old men will dream dreams. Acts 2:17

Not all dreams are from God, but when they are, usually there is clarity and they <u>never</u> go against God's Word. There is a sense in your spirit that it was from God. It would be dangerous to base the direction of your life on dreams or visions, but that does not negate the fact that God speaks to His children through dreams. He has in the past and He does today.

God has given dreams of warning to reveal the enemy's plans ahead of time so that we can pray and thwart those plans. These are dreams given for the purpose of intercession. Should God use you in this capacity, take these dreams and visions very seriously and pray until the answer comes. You may want to keep your journal or a Dictaphone near your bed. Otherwise, by morning you may have forgotten what He spoke to your heart.

A Warning in the Night

*I*t was in November of 2002. In the middle of the night, I was fast asleep, deep in a dream and yet my spirit was wide awake. As the dream unfolded, I could hear the phone ring and the person on the other end said, "Your son, Jacob, has just died." Even though I was still asleep, I started to grieve because I wasn't sure of his relationship with God. Startled, I awoke from my dream.

This was one of those dreams that I knew was from God. I was familiar with God speaking to me in dreams for the purpose of intercession. I did not share this with my son because I didn't want to put fear in him. There are some things that God shares with you that are meant just for you.

Knowing the seriousness of this assignment, I did enlist several trusted intercessors to pray with me. You see, one can put 1000 to flight and two can put 10,000 to flight (Deut. 32:30).

So for the next seven months I laid hold of my covenant with God and prayed God's promises consistently for my son's protection, coming against premature death and for my son's relationship with the Lord. At the end of the sixth month, Jacob had chest pain and went to the ER. This was not a new occurrence in his life but the doctors had never found anything seriously wrong with his heart. So, being reminded once again of this dream, I felt the need to share it with him. He took it to heart and in the next few weeks informed me that he had prayed a few times, which encouraged me greatly. But I still continued to pray. Then in the seventh month, around 8:00 PM, the phone rang. But instead of it being the person in my dream, it was my son, Jacob.

He said, "Mom I was on my motorcycle not wearing a helmet, traveling over 35 miles an hour when an oncoming vehicle with a semi behind her decided to turn into a road in front of me. She didn't slow much because of the semi. Not seeing me, she turned into me, hitting me head-on. My bike crashed into her car and landed on her hood. A bystander said that it looked like I was thrown 20 feet into the air. I did a summersault and landed on my butt next to her car. I got up and took my bike off of her car. Mom, I felt like I was flying on angel's wings!"

I said, "You were, Jacob, that's the power of prayer. What were you thinking when you were in the air?"

He said, "I said the death prayer, 'God forgive me, Jesus be in my heart!'"

God met my son when he was hanging between heaven and earth. Amazingly he had no broken bones, no ripped clothes, just a few aches and pains.

Because I was praying faithfully, God's angels were already on the scene of the accident. Jacobs's heart was receptive to the voice of the Holy Spirit as he faced death. I heard God's voice of warning. As I joined Him in what He was doing and prayed the Scripture promises, God dispatched His angels. I was not battling alone. Halleluiah!

As I prayed God's Word, His angels went forth and destroyed Satan's plans for Jacob. The angels were already there, waiting for Jacob before Jacob ever arrived on the scene. How do I know this?

> Bless the LORD, you His angels, mighty in strength, who perform His word, obeying the voice of His word!   Psalm 103:20 (NASB)

I used my voice to pray God's promises of protection, deliverance and salvation over Jacob. As I used my voice to speak God's Word, the angels of God obeyed God's Word. I was literally putting a sword in the angels' hands as in Eph. 6:17, they stood ALERT AND READY to do battle.

$\mathcal{H}$ow do you know when to stop praying? If your spiritual ears are sensitive to God's voice, you will know. He will give you release:

- Let the peace of God rule in your heart (Col. 3:15). The word "rule" in the Amplified says, "act as an umpire." Pray until you have peace.

- When the burden lifts.

- God may give you a word or a scripture informing you that the answer has come.

- At other times, you just know that He has you praying and you continue to pray, by faith, until the answer comes.

This was the case here. I knew that this was so vital that even though I did not see anything happening in the natural as I prayed for seven months, I did not let up. Many people miss God because they don't see an answer right away and they quit too soon. **Persevering in prayer is one of the greatest keys to victory against the forces of darkness.**

Not all dreams are from God. But when they are, you'll know because they're revealed for a divine purpose. The same goes for visions.

Visions

$\mathcal{A}$ vision is a picture, still or moving, that you see while you are awake. God opens your spiritual eyes and gives you a visual aid, showing you how to pray. You may not even know the person that God directs you to pray for. Even though you may never meet them in your lifetime, because you are joining God in prayer for them, you can be certain that God is moving in their lives.

> ...If there is a prophet among you, I, the Lord, shall make Myself known to him in a vision. I shall speak with him in a dream. Numbers 12:6 (NASB)

> Indeed God speaks once, or twice, yet no one notices it. In a dream, a vision of the night, when sound sleep falls on men, while they slumber in their beds, then He opens the ears of men, and seals their instruction, Job 33:14-16 (NASB)

Seek God and don't limit Him in the way He chooses to speak to you. Just heed His voice when He does.

If God shows you something prophetically about your prodigal, He is already on the scene waiting for you to join Him in prayer. As you pray faithfully, He will work mightily in your wayward loved one's life. God's Word always comes with the power to fulfill it!

If it does not come to pass right away, keep praying. Several years ago, God gave me a vision of someone I knew standing on a boat with men surrounding her. I knew that God was asking me to pray for her protection. So I interceded daily not knowing when or where she would ever be standing on a boat. I shared it with her and months later she took a job working in the shipyards. After a few weeks, the harassment started.

But there was no need to fear! God gave me a prayer directive months before and the work was already accomplished in the spiritual realm. The incidents were reported and the men were fired immediately! God's protection was upon her.

So even if you do not fully understand when God gives you a vision, take it seriously and be faithful to pray. We do not seek after visions, but that does not negate the fact that God still speaks to His people this way. Seek after God! For if you seek Him with all your heart, you will find Him!

SOWING SEEDS

*I*t is very important that you record what you are hearing from God. Have you ever looked at a garden journal? They are a very thorough record of the gardener's progress. Below you will find a list of what an earthly garden journal might contain.

- Graph of Garden Plot
- Condition of Soil
- Cultivation Process
- Seeds Planted - Seed Depth
- Light Source
- Water
- Pest Problems, Damage and Solutions
- Success Rate
- Disease Problems
- Fertilizer
- Growth
- Maturity
- Harvest
- Yield
- Overview of Year
- Future Plans, Thoughts and Reflections

If earthly gardeners see such value of having a plan and making sure that they follow through to ensure success, we must too. For the garden that we till will reap eternal rewards – souls. Using the forms in the back of this prayer guide will help you create a plan. If you haven't used them yet, give them a try.

Journal what God brings to light and date each entry. This is important, as in time you might forget the details. Every detail is important! Journaling what God reveals will cement it in your heart and give you further direction as you pray.

> And the Lord answered me and said, "Write the vision and engrave it so plainly upon tablets that everyone who passes may [be able to] read [it easily and quickly] as he hastens by."
> Habakkuk 2:2 (AMP)

Pray until God releases you from the burden. Praying for any length is not about begging God to do something; rather it is about bathing this person or situation in God's promises until the seed of His Word takes root and His will is birthed on the earth.

Prayer Journal:

I keep a recorder or a journal next to my bed. If God gives me a dream or a vision in the middle of the night, I record it. I have learned from experience that if I do not do this, by morning I have forgotten important details. When God gives you a vision or a dream it is important to pray immediately. He is asking you to join Him NOW. He is on the scene **now** waiting for you to join Him.

Pray until God releases you from the burden. This could take a few minutes or it may become an ongoing prayer directive lasting longer than a year. Be faithful to pray it through. When God gives you a dream or a vision for the purpose of prayer, write it on your prayer page as well as on the page of the person you are praying for. This will help you to pray consistently until you see God's answer. Be sure to date every entry. Tonight when you go to bed, put your journal and a pen or your recorder on your nightstand. Expect God to lead you in prayer.

> And he saw that there was no man, and wondered that there was no intercessor …
> Isaiah 59:16 (KJV)

Spiritual Disciplines

Fasting

*G*od can use fasting to:

- Loose the bands of wickedness
- Undo heavy burdens
- Let the oppressed go free
- Break every yoke!

The course of our wayward loved ones can be changed through fasting and prayer! God desires to loosen the bands that are holding them captive and set them free.

> Is not this the fast that I have chosen? To loose the bands of wickedness, to undo the heavy burdens, and to let the oppressed go free, and that ye break every yoke?
> Isaiah 58:6 (KJV)

In the book of Daniel we see that Daniel realized it was time for God's people to come out of exile back to Jerusalem. He set His face to seek the Lord and clothed himself in sackcloth and ashes as he interceded on behalf of the people. Daniel fasted and prayed for the Jews to be set free! Let's learn from his example!

1. He confessed the peoples' sins:

> We have sinned and have committed iniquity, and have done wickedly, and have rebelled, even by departing from thy precepts and from thy judgment:
> Daniel 9:5 (KJV)

2. He cried out to God to turn away His anger and be merciful to this people:

> O Lord, in keeping with all your righteous acts, turn away your anger and your wrath from Jerusalem, your city, your holy hill. Our sins and the iniquities of our fathers have made Jerusalem and your people an object of scorn to all those around us.
> Daniel 9:16

3. He pleaded with God for forgiveness:

> O Lord, listen! O Lord, forgive! O Lord, hear and act! For your sake, O my God, do not delay, because your city and your people bear your Name.
> Daniel 9:19

His prayer, coupled with fasting, was powerful! A decree was given that all the Jews were free to go back to Jerusalem to build the Temple.

Fasting is not about persuading God, but enjoined with prayer will bring you to the place where you can:

1. Hear God more clearly
2. Increase your faith
3. Pray expectantly and powerfully
4. Be in tune with God
5. Gain direction
6. Hit the mark in prayer

Fasting can increase your ability to hear the voice of the Holy Spirit.

> While they were worshiping the Lord and fasting, the Holy Spirit said...
> Acts 13:2

Jesus spoke of fasting. When He did, He didn't say, "if" we fast, but rather "when" we fast. (Matthew 6:16)

Fasting is, or should be, a regular part of the life of a Christian. For some this may be a new experience.

There are no rules. What you do is between you and God. Here are a few suggestions to get you started:

- **The Traditional Fast** – refraining from eating all food. You may still drink water or other fluids, as led by God.

- **The Partial Fast** – This means omitting a specific meal from your diet or refraining from certain types of foods, such as the "Daniel Fast" found in Daniel 10.

> At that time I, Daniel, mourned for three weeks. I ate no choice food; no meat or wine touched my lips; and I used no lotions at all until the three weeks were over.
> Daniel 10:2-3

> Please test your servants for ten days: Give us nothing but vegetables to eat and water to drink.
> Daniel 1:12

Pray and ask the Lord for direction. If you have a health condition, consider fasting from certain activities or a favorite food. Before you fast, discuss it with your doctor.

Follow Daniel's example of prayer, plead your prodigal's case before the throne of God. Ask God to not only forgive your sins, but the sins of your prodigals as well. Remember Daniel prayed, "We" not "They."

> We have sinned and have committed iniquity, and have done wickedly, and have rebelled, even by departing from thy precepts and from thy judgments.
>
> Daniel 9:5 (KJV)

Lord, give us a heart to know You, that we might return to You with all of our hearts. (Jer. 24:7) This I pray in Jesus' name.

SOWING SEEDS

*W*hen Jesus' disciples failed in their attempt to cast out a deaf and dumb spirit from a child, the father of the child went to Jesus to ask Him to cast it out. After Jesus rebuked the demon, it came out. Later His disciples asked Him why they weren't able to cast it out like they had done so many times before. Jesus answered them saying, "This kind does not go out except by prayer and fasting." (Matt. 17:21)

At times, Jesus may lead you to add fasting to your prayers. Fasting may be the determining factor to your breakthrough.

Prayer Journal:

Don't be discouraged if you do not see results immediately. God is at work deep within their heart. Remember, we can't always see what is going on under the surface of the heart. There have been times that I have sought God and it wasn't until I fasted that my answer came. Ask God if and when you should fast. Journal what happens.

In the book of Joel we find Israel in sin. The Lord says in Joel 2:12-13 (MSG) ... it's not too late – come back to me and really mean it! Come fasting and weeping, sorry for your sins!" Change your life ... and here's why: God is kind and merciful. He takes a deep breath, puts up with a lot, this most patient God, extravagant in love, always ready to cancel catastrophe.

Who knows? Maybe He'll do it now ... declare a day of repentance, a holy fasting (Joel 2:2-14, 15).

> I will pour out my Spirit on every kind of people. Your sons will prophesy, also your daughters, your old men will dream, your young men will see visions. I'll even pour out my spirit on the servants, men and women both.   Joel 2:28-29 (MSG)

God poured out revival after they fasted. Fasting will prepare the way for a fresh manifestation of God's presence in the lives of your loved ones.

Kingdom Authority

*Y*ou have the capacity and power to touch millions of people through your prayers. As you do, you and those whom you are praying for will need God's protection. One day when we get to heaven, we'll be amazed at the tools God provided that were never used. So don't wait any longer, pick up your garden tools today and become familiar with them.

Authority

*W*hen Jesus redeemed us from sin at the cross and triumphantly rose again from the dead, He won the victory:

> And having spoiled principalities and powers, he made a shew of them openly, triumphing over them in it.   Colossians 2:15 (KJV)

The Greek definition for "spoiled" means, "to totally strip of power and to undress." Jesus stripped wicked principalities and powers of their authority, jurisdiction, liberty, power, right and strength to work in the Christian's life. However, even though the enemy is powerless against you, he uses deception to convince you otherwise. That is why it is important to know, believe and act upon the truth of God's Word. It dispels the enemy's lies.

When you are empowered by the Holy Spirit, you can declare that anything trying to hinder God's kingdom in their heart is forbidden and powerless. You can confidently claim that your prodigals are loosed from Satan's hold.

You can pray like this:

Father, I take the authority that You have given me and I appropriate what You have done and I declare that powers and principalities are spoiled, totally stripped of their power over _____ and rendered useless. In Jesus' Name.

SOWING SEEDS

> For our struggle is not against flesh and blood, but against the rulers, against the authorities, against the powers of this dark world and against the spiritual forces of evil in the heavenly realms.   Eph. 6:12

*T*his battle is not a matter of choice but a fact. Satan's forces are fighting whether or not you fight back. Make no mistake about it; you are in a spiritual war.

There is a battle going on in the heavenlies for the hearts of your loved ones. To remain ignorant or to refuse to fight back will guarantee defeat.

Sometimes the enemy doesn't want to give up his hold easily. Sometimes circumstances begin to look worse. It is here where you will have to take hold of God's promise and stand. When it seems that all hell breaks loose, when everything seems to be falling apart, hold your ground with naked faith. When the storm subsides you will find that you are the one still standing. Do not give up when the battle gets tough. Appropriate the victory that Christ has already won. With knees deep in mud, go in and take the land of the heart for Christ. No matter how treacherous Satan may appear, you can always be one step ahead of him – for you have the Holy Spirit. But your heart must be sensitive to His voice.

Prayer Journal:

Use the following prompt to talk to God about what you are going through.

Father, thank You for going before me. I take my place in this battle and I hold on to Your victory...

The Kingdom of God

𝒴our wayward loved ones are those whose thoughts are taken captive by the enemy. But God has given **you** the tools to set them free and to bring the kingdom of God into their lives.

Jesus said,

> "I will give you the keys of the kingdom of heaven; whatever you bind on earth will be bound in heaven, and whatever you loose on earth will be loosed in heaven."
> Matthew 16:19

> Or how can one enter a strong man's house and plunder his goods, unless he first binds the strong man? And then he will plunder his house. Matthew 12:29 (NKJ)

The Kingdom of God is anywhere that God has rule. It involves His Lordship and the power and activity of the Holy Spirit. According to Luke 17:21 (AMP) the kingdom of God is within your heart. God wants to set up His kingdom in our hearts.

Through your prayers, you can usher in the kingdom of God – <u>His very presence</u> – into the hearts of your loved ones. This is vital because unless they are experiencing His presence, they will not return; for Christianity will be just another form of religion to them. When God's presence is manifested, there is freedom (2 Cor. 3:17). And there is growth!

> "How can we picture God's kingdom? What kind of story can we use? It's like a pine nut. When it lands on the ground it is quite small as seeds go, yet once it is planted it grows into a huge pine tree with thick branches. Eagles nest in it."
> Mark 4:30-32 (MSG)

Your prodigals still have a free will and must make the decision to surrender for themselves, but your prayers will open the door for God to soften their hearts and remove the veil, making it easier for them to surrender.

Satan desires to set up his kingdom in the hearts of God's people. I am not talking about possession, because Christians cannot be possessed by evil spirits. But Satan wants to rule their lives by influencing and oppressing them. He knows that as a man "thinks in his heart, so he is." (Proverbs 23:7) So he constantly tries to plant his evil thoughts into their hearts.

Stay close to God. He can – and will – reveal the enemy's plans. God goes before you! I have had numerous experiences when the Lord showed me specifically how to pray for my wayward loved ones, what the strongholds were, and revealed the enemy's plan so that I could join Him in prayer.

He goes before you!

Binding and Loosing

*T*hrough the spiritual weapons of binding and loosing you can forbid Satan's activity from your loved ones' lives and pray in God's kingdom. Now listen closely again to what Jesus said:

> I will give you the keys of the kingdom of heaven; and whatever you bind (declare to be improper and unlawful) on earth must be what is already bound in heaven; and whatever you loose (declare lawful) on earth must be what is already loosed in heaven.   Matthew 16:19 (AMP)

Isn't that exciting? God has equipped you with the keys that will set your loved ones free. But in order for them to work, you must use them! Let's take a closer look at these keys of binding and loosing. The Hebrew word for "bind" in this scripture means, "To tie or join together." I can bind or tie the truth of God's Word to the hearts of my loved ones.

In the Greek, to "bind" means, "to tie, to forbid." When the Holy Spirit reveals darkness, you can bind it, tie it up and forbid it. Now, I am not suggesting that you walk around constantly trying to bind everything or equate everything you see with evil spirits. It is important to be led by God when you use these tools.

When Jesus redeemed us from sin at the cross and triumphantly rose again from the dead, He defeated Satan at the cross (Col. 2:15); He stripped wicked principalities and powers of their authority, jurisdiction, liberty, power, right and strength to work in the Christian's life. Satan is powerless against us unless **we** open the door to him.

Your wayward loved ones will not take authority over the evil that is coming against their lives. Therefore, you must do this for them. You have the legal right and authority to bind and forbid what has already been bound and forbidden in heaven. Satan's jurisdiction – liberty, power, right and strength – has been bound in heaven, so you can bind it here on earth. (Matt. 16:19)

The word "loose" here in the Greek means, "to untie, unbind, destroy or dissolve." When people are oppressed and bound up, you can loose and untie them from these things through prayer. For example, God's Word tells us that,

> For he rescued us from the domain of darkness, and transferred us to the kingdom of His beloved Son.   Colossians 1:13 (NASB)

In the spiritual realm, your loved ones have already been loosed from the power of darkness. So you can loose them from demonic oppression with your prayers as the Holy Spirit leads us. Once you do this you can bind their hearts to God's Word.

O My son, keep your father's [God-given] commandment and forsake not the law of [God] your mother [taught you]. Bind them continually upon your heart and tie them about your neck.

Proverbs 6:20-21 (AMP)

As the Holy Spirit leads you, pray like this:

By the authority of the name of Jesus Christ, I declare that the spirit of destruction is bound inoperable against _____ according to God's word. The spirit that is trying to destroy my loved one is rendered powerless.

I bind_____ 's heart to God's promise that says that she/he shall know the truth and the truth shall set her/him free!

Resist the evil spirits that are coming against your loved ones. We do not chase demons, but if God reveals one, we can resist him and he must flee.

When you pray for your loved ones, the Holy Spirit hovers over them and is constantly at work pulling down their walls of resistance in order to set up God's kingdom — His rule there. As He hovers over them, He will warn you of impending danger so that you can join Him as a watchman of their heart.

But be sure that Christ is Lord of your heart and that you are under His authority before you use these keys. Allow Him to set up His kingdom in your heart so that His authority can flow forth from your prayers.

The only authority that you have comes from Christ's authority as you submit to Him.

The Blood of Jesus

*A*re you pleading the blood of Jesus over your family daily? If not, don't wait any longer! It is God's provision of protection, deliverance and salvation for them. Jesus Christ poured out His blood for your salvation and your deliverance. He paid a tremendous price. You must not take that for granted. He gave His life for your salvation and the freedom of your family.

Let's take a look in the Old Testament to get a picture of how the blood applied saves families.

Moses was called by God to deliver the children of Israel out of bondage. God performed many miracles, revealing to Pharaoh that He was moving on behalf of Israel. But Pharaoh refused to listen because His heart was hardened. So Moses warned that an angel of death would come and slay the first born in every house. The children of Israel were the only ones that would escape; if they followed the Lord's instruction. They must take a lamb, kill it and apply it to the side and upper doorposts of their houses. The term used was, a lamb for a house. Once the lamb's blood was applied, every person inside that house would be safe. (Ex. 12:1-13)

*J*esus Christ is the Lamb for your house today. Apply His blood through prayer for protection and deliverance. **Where the blood is applied, the destroyer cannot come in.**

Plead the blood of Jesus over your loved ones for their salvation, deliverance and protection. There is power in the blood of the Lamb, Jesus Christ!

> And they overcame him because of the blood of the lamb and the word of our testimonies.   Revelation 12:11 (NASB)

Be determined not to leave one member of your family in the kingdom of darkness.

God has made you a priest unto Himself.

> But ye are a chosen generation, a royal priesthood, a holy nation, a peculiar people; that ye should shew forth the praises of him who hath called you out of darkness into his marvelous light;   1 Peter 2:9 (KJV)

> …To Him who loved us and washed us from our sins in His own blood, and has made us kings and priests to His God and Father, to Him be glory and dominion forever and ever. Amen.   Revelation 1:5-6 (NKJV)

Priests in the Old Testament were in charge of sprinkling the blood. You, as a New Testament believer priest, are in charge of sprinkling the blood of Jesus over your loved ones hearts and lives through prayer.

We do not fight against flesh and blood.

> For our struggle is not against flesh and blood, but against the rulers, against the authorities, against the powers of this dark world and against the spiritual forces of evil in the heavenly realms.   Ephesians 6:12

This is a spiritual battle requiring spiritual weapons. As you sprinkle the blood, demonic spirits will flee! How do you do this? Just very simply, pray.

Prayer Journal:

Pray over your wayward loved ones and appropriate the Blood of Jesus over their lives.

Lord, I cover my loved ones with Your blood. I plead the blood of Jesus for Peace, (Col. 1:20), salvation and the forgiveness of sin (Eph. 1:7). Through the blood we overcome Satan and put him to flight (Rev. 12:11), in Jesus name Amen.

Empowered With the Holy Spirit

*E*very Christian has the Holy Spirit, but not every Christian is fully surrendered to Him. As you yield your life to Him, He will pray through you and empower you.

> In the same way, the Spirit helps us in our weakness. We do not know what we ought to pray for, but the Spirit himself intercedes for us with groans that words cannot express.   Romans 8:26

The Holy Spirit is the one who helps you when you pray; not only praying through you, but also **empowering you and warning you when danger is approaching.** He is the one who frees souls. Ask Him to give you a fresh infilling of His presence.

Do you want to bring your prodigals home? Then not only must you pray, but you must be filled with the Holy Ghost and walk in His anointing!

> ... Not by might nor by power, but by my Spirit, says the LORD Almighty.
>   Zechariah 4:6

The Holy Spirit is the One Who will reveal what is in a heart so that you can pray effectively. Be sensitive to Him at all times.

Man has a free will, but your prayers allow God to move more freely upon their hearts. Scripture tells us in the book of James that we do not have because we do not ask, so ask! Don't give up. Stand strong, for God, "is able to do exceedingly above all that you ask or think." (Ephesians 3:20)

Be sensitive to the Holy Spirit's leading and don't push doors open. Wait for God to open doors. Walk in readiness and continue cultivating hearts so that they will be receptive when you have the opportunity to speak.

Your victory in this battle is not dependent on your own strength. You can wage war clothed in the power of Almighty God! King David said,

> For Thou hast girded me with strength for battle; Thou hast subdued under me those who rose up against me.   Psalm 18:39 (NASB)

The battle is the Lords! He goes before you! He has girded you with His power for the battle. Allow Him to lead you however He chooses. If you follow Him, you are guaranteed victory because He has already won it.

*P*ay attention! God wants to empower you with His Spirit so that you can join Him in the fight for souls. He wants to manifest Himself to you!

> The person who has My commandments and keeps them is the one who [really] loves Me; and whoever [really] loves Me will be loved by My Father, and I [too] will love him and will show, (reveal, manifest) myself to him. [I will let Myself be clearly seen by him and make Myself real to Him.]   John 14:21 (AMP)

Prayer Journal:

Do you want God to manifest Himself to you so you can pray effectively? Then walk in obedience to Him.

> In the same way, the Spirit helps us in our weakness. We do not know what we ought to pray for, but the Spirit himself intercedes for us with groans that words cannot express. And he who searches our hearts knows the mind of the Spirit, because the Spirit intercedes for the saints in accordance with God's will.
> Romans 8:26-27

The word, "help," in the Greek means, "to take hold of, together with." When you pray in the Spirit, He literally takes hold of the circumstances, leading you, empowering you and interceding through you.

Father, I surrender everything to You. Show me if am walking in disobedience to You. Reveal Yourself to me. Baptize me afresh with Your Spirit.

Write what He shows you in your journal and your response. Be sensitive to the Holy Spirit and He will pray through you.

> Not by might nor by power, but by My Spirit, says the LORD of hosts.
> Zechariah 4:6 (NASB)

Pray and Write !

The Gardeners Protection

> For our struggle is not against flesh and blood, but against the rulers, against the authorities, against the powers of this dark world and against the spiritual forces of evil in the heavenly realms.
> Ephesians 6:12

*F*or your protection against the evil one, the Master Gardener has supplied you with special attire. However, it is only effective when worn. Even as a gardener wears protective clothing to guard himself from harmful elements such as the sun and insects; you, the heart gardener, must protect yourself as well.

Earthly gardeners know how important it is to dress properly before going out to work in their garden. The hazards are many, from sunstroke to mosquitoes, to briars, thorns and predators.

Being underdressed and defenseless is a sure way to neglect your garden, allowing all kinds of predators to enter.

You can be fully equipped so when predators show up and see you covered with Christ, they won't stand a chance. Yes, the Master Gardener has supplied you with supernatural tools, but you must choose to wear them in order to be completely effective.

> Put on the full armor of God so that you can take your stand against the devil's schemes.
> Ephesians 6:11

This armor is symbolic of Christ as your covering. In essence, you climb into the very armor of God when fully submitted to Christ. When the evil one looks at you, he will see you covered with the righteousness and victory of Christ. He trembles in fear for he sees Jesus who rendered him powerless.

As you cast off the deeds of darkness and boldly wear God's armor, your life becomes hidden in His. From the top of your head to the soles of your feet, you are protected and share the victory with Jesus. Does this mean you will never have any bad thing happen to you? No. It means you are equipped to overcome <u>whatever</u> happens!

Embrace the victory Christ won for you at the cross even though unseen. Embrace it until it is realized in this natural world in answer to your prayers.

By daily arraying yourself in the armor of God and praying His Word, you will always be prepared for the attacks of the enemy.

> ... do not be afraid of the enemy; [earnestly] remember the Lord and imprint Him [on your minds], great and terrible, and [take from Him courage to] fight for your brethren, your sons, your daughters, your wives, and your homes.   Nehemiah 4:14 (AMP)

> And that about wraps it up. God is strong, and he wants you strong. So take everything the Master has set out for you, well-made weapons of the best materials. And put them to use so you will be able to stand up to everything the Devil throws your way. This is no afternoon athletic contest that we'll walk away from and forget about in a couple of hours. This is for keeps, a life-or-death fight to the finish against the Devil and all his angels. Be prepared. You're up against far more than you can handle on your own. Take all the help you can get, every weapon God has issued, so that when it's all over but the shouting you'll still be on your feet. Truth, righteousness, peace, faith, and salvation are more than words. Learn how to apply them. You'll need them throughout your life. God's Word is an indispensable weapon. In the same way, prayer is essential in this ongoing warfare. Pray hard and long. Pray for your brothers and sisters. Keep your eyes open. Keep each other's spirits up so that no one falls behind or drops out.   Ephesians 6:10-18 (MSG)

* Go to the SEED portion of your journal to put on the Armor of God.

SOWING SEEDS

*B*ut spiritual warfare is not just a matter of prayer. Did you know that your

very life is spiritual warfare? Prayer is more than words. When you are full of the Holy Ghost, His presence in you pushes back the darkness, and your life becomes a weapon in the hands of God. Your very life overcomes evil with good. When you walk out of your prayer closet, the presence of Christ in you will expose, convict and reprove others without you ever saying a word.

> Take no part in and have no fellowship with the fruitless deeds and enterprises of darkness, but instead [let your lives be so in contrast as to] expose and reprove and convict them.   Ephesians 5:11 (AMP)

This is one of the most powerful forms of spiritual warfare. Your life is a weapon!

> and do not go on presenting the members of your body to sin {as} instruments of unrighteousness; but present yourselves to God as those alive from the dead, and your members as instruments of righteousness to God.   Romans 6:13 (NASB)

"Instruments" in the Greek is "weapons." We are to offer ourselves as weapons of righteousness.

There is no doubt about it. Your life is spiritual warfare! Do you want to win your lost loved ones? Do you want to bring your prodigals home? Then not only must you pray, but you must be filled with the Holy Ghost and walk in His anointing! Unless your walk matches your talk, they will never take you seriously and they will surely not want what you have! I am not talking about perfection here. Spirituality is not about being perfect or never failing. It is about being real before others and before God. It is about letting His life live through you.

Do not be overcome by evil, but overcome evil with good. Romans 12:21

A gentle answer turns away wrath, but a harsh word stirs up anger.
Proverbs 15:1

Prayer Journal:

Use the following prompt to journal your prayer to God.

Father, I totally surrender to You. I offer up my body to You as an instrument of righteousness. Live through me, in Jesus Name.

_____
_____
_____
_____
_____
_____
_____
_____
_____
_____
_____
_____
_____
_____
_____
_____
_____
_____
_____
_____
_____
_____
_____
_____
_____
_____

Pray and Write !

Abiding in the Vine

Connected to the Vine

> "Abide in Me, and I in you. As the branch cannot bear fruit of itself, unless it abides in the vine, neither can you, unless you abide in Me. I am the Vine, you are the branches. He who abides in Me, and I in him, bears much fruit; for without Me you can do nothing."
>
> John 15:4-5 (NKJV)

*J*esus died so that He could live in you and through you by His Holy Spirit. You don't have to struggle to have an abiding relationship with Him. He's only a whisper away, for Jesus is as near as your heart. When you seek to be led by His Spirit, you'll receive what you need for each day. As you stay connected to the Vine, His life-giving power will flow through you.

Yield yourself and start talking to Him. He's waiting to pour out His grace and love upon you so you can be a conduit of His love to others. As you maintain this living communion with Him, He'll work in and through you to accomplish His will and purposes for your life.

> If you abide in Me, and My words abide in you, you will ask what you desire, and it shall be done for you.
>
> John 15:7 (NKJ)

Abiding in Christ is one of the greatest keys to answered prayer. For as you maintain an intimate relationship with Him and hide His Word in your heart, you hold the very thoughts and intentions of His heart. Then your prayers will flow directly from the heart of God. And He says that if you ask anything according to His will, He hears you and you have those requests.

To "abide" means, "to maintain a relationship of fellowship and obedience with Him."

As you walk in obedience by offering your 'self- life' on the altar, your fleshly desires die, and the exquisite aroma of the Christ life comes forth as a sweet fragrance to God. His fragrance will then flow throughout your garden and into every garden that you walk through. It is a fragrance more beautiful than any found in earthly gardens, and it is only found in the garden of the heart that is yielded to Him.

*R*emember, the fragrance in your life comes through intimacy, not performance. Therefore, do not fall into the trap of trying to get all of your "prayers in" so that you can pat yourself on the back. For in all your **doing**, you will find yourself no longer **hearing** His voice. You must seek His face with **ALL** your heart.

Recently the Lord said to me, "Do not be so consumed with the work that I have given you to do, that you are no longer consumed with Me."

You must be consumed with Him and hearing His voice. Are you? The very life of your garden depends on it. For truly… APART FROM HIM YOU CAN DO NOTHING!

Prayer Journal:

Spend some time today journaling about your relationship with the Lord. Talk to Him about your prayer life. Are you relating to Him during your quiet time or are you just "trying to get all your prayers in?" There is a big difference. One speaks of relationship and the other speaks of works. Aim towards an intimate relationship. Power in prayer comes from intimacy with God.

Pruning

"I am the true vine, and My Father is the vinedresser. Every branch in Me that does not bear fruit, He takes away; and every {branch} that bears fruit, He prunes it, that it may bear more fruit."   John 15:1-2 (NASB)

*H*ave you ever watched someone prune a grapevine as woody stalks and leafy branches are cut away? You'd think they were trying to kill it by their hacking away. But in reality, if left alone, the excess foliage and dead canes only hinder the growth of the grapes. Grape plants have a tendency to produce new branches, but no fruit. Without pruning, the vine will become so dense with luxurious leaves and shoots that the sun won't be able to reach the area where the fruit should form. The plant's vigorous growth is deceiving from a distance, for it looks like there is a great abundance of fruit, but up close there's a disappointing harvest.

As an intercessor, it is important that God prunes away all the traces of your old self-life, so that He can move freely through you. Regular pruning is essential for the production of abundant fruit. In a spiritual sense, the pruning process cuts away all that remains of the self-life. The activities, priorities and preoccupations that drain time and energy from a more significant ministry for God must go also. What is God asking you to let go of? Write what He reveals on a journaling page. He is asking you to relinquish things that keep you from fulfilling the greater purpose He has for you.

His pruning is not done randomly, however. He works uniquely in each person. What He considers needless in my life might be necessary in yours. Pruning is all about denying the desires of the flesh to allow the spirit to grow.

The goal is not to harm you, but that you bear much fruit — the inner fruit that produces a Christ-likeness in you, and the outward fruit that brings glory to Him.

> ... "By this is My Father is glorified, that you bear much fruit, and {so} prove to be My disciples."
> John 15:8 (NASB)

The Gardener's care for you doesn't stop with pruning. As branches become heavy-laden with fruit, they'll follow their natural tendency to trail down and grow along the ground. There the fruit will become coated with dirt and dust, and when it rains; the fruit will get muddy and mildewed. If left alone, the fruit will rot. So the vinedresser lifts up each fruit-bearing branch and ties it to a trellis, and then washes it with water to remove the dirt.

In a similar manner even when you're fruitful, you'll still experience defilement from your contact with the world. Just like the dirty ground remains under the vine, so your fleshly desires are always waiting for you to be reckoned with daily. But the Master, the "lifter of your head" (Ps. 3:3), has provided His Word to wash you like a gardener washes the branches.

Washing with the Water of the Word

> ... Christ also loved the church and gave Himself up for her; that He might sanctify her, having cleansed her by the washing of water with the word. Ephesians 5:25-26 (NASB)

*7*s life going so well for you that you've relaxed your time in God's Word? Being fruitful is not the time to be neglectful. Be on your guard, for within moments, a peaceful home can turn into a dirty battlefield if you're not careful.

A little argument turned into a shouting match between my husband, Geno, and me. One thing led to another until yelling turned to silence. First an hour, then a day, eventually a week passed without a word between us. Because of our stubborn hard hearts, we distanced ourselves from God and refused to read His Word. But God waited patiently to ... sprinkle clean water on us and make us clean ... (Ezekiel 36:25)

After a week I could take no more. Sitting at my kitchen counter, I hesitantly opened my Bible to John.

> "A new commandment I give to you, that you love one another, even as I have loved you, that you also love one another."
>
> John 13:34 (NASB)

I turned the page and He poured out John 14:15,

> "If you love Me, keep My commandments."
>
> John 14:15 (NASB)

Then He spoke to my heart, "The issue is not between you and your husband. The issue is between you and Me. If you love Me, you will keep My commandments and My command is that you love him."

For the first time in a week, I saw clearly. My heart was washed with the Word. I humbly went to my husband to share God's Word with Him. The Lord gently lifted us up, washed us off with the water of His Word, and cleansed us from the defilement of our fleshly nature.

> Now ye are clean through the Word which I have spoken unto you.
>
> John 15:3 (KJV)

♥ Author's Note: For further instruction, purchase our journal "Washing with the Word."

SOWING SEEDS

*W*hen you feel dirty from allowing your old nature to rule, or through contact with the world, read Scripture and allow it to speak to your situation. Now, change your mind and attitude to God and turn to Him, so He can cleanse away your sins and send you wonderful times of refreshment from the presence of the Lord.

Prayer Journal:

Find Bible verses that pertain to your circumstances and receive them into your heart, permitting His Word to cleanse you. Turn the scripture into a prayer to God. Then record what He speaks to your heart.

Letting Go and Letting God

Commit your way to the LORD, Trust also in Him, and He will do it.

Psalm 37:5 (NASB)

*O*nce you have made your prayer requests, it's easy to take them back by fretting and worrying about the situation instead of trusting God for the answer. Holding on too tightly squelches God's answers. Let me explain.

When we were on family vacation, my three-year-old son, Jacob, came running into the cabin with a tight fist.

"Mommy, I caught a tree frog."

His little hand slowly opened to give me a peek. But to his dismay, the frog was limp and motionless. He hung onto it so tightly; the life was squeezed right out of it.

How tightly are you holding on to situations you've prayed about and said you've put into God's hands? Sometimes it's hard to leave your requests with God, isn't it? After all, you really do care about these things and you hang on tightly, somehow thinking you can help God. Maybe you feel you can't trust Him with it. Or, maybe it's your lack of faith.

Whatever your reason is, if you don't release it to Him, your tight grasp will restrain God from working. He is faithful. He loves you. He desires to bless you, and He wants to answer your prayers. So surrender all to Him — your family, your possessions, your finances, your health, your ministry, your very life and all the situations you're praying for. Put them into His hands, giving Him permission to do whatever it takes to bear fruit. Let go, and let God do the work.

Let him have all your worries and cares, for he is always thinking about you and watching everything that concerns you. 1 Peter 5:7 (TLB)

Prayer Journal:

Heavenly Father, I give this situation to You, once and for all. I'll continue to pray and wait expectantly for Your answer to come to pass. Help me not to fret, but to trust You.

Prayer of Committal

Dear Father, I commit (name of person or situation) to You and deposit
_____ to Your charge, entrusting him/her to Your care. I know that the plans You
have for _____ are not to harm him/her, but to prosper him; plans to give
him/her hope and a future. You are able to do immeasurably more than I could
ever ask or imagine according to the power that works within me. Nothing is too
difficult for You, so I release _____ to You. In Jesus name I pray. Amen. (Acts
20:32 (AMP), Jer. 29:11 & 32:17, Eph. 3:20)

Time

> There is a time for everything, and a season for every activity under heaven ... a
> time to plant and a time to uproot,   Ecclesiastes 3:1-2

*7*ime is a valuable garden tool supplied by the Master. How we use it will

determine our garden's outcome. We can reminisce about our flourishing gardens of
the past or daydream about exquisite gardens of the future, but reality is **NOW**.
What we do today will be the reality of tomorrow's harvest. Each gardener is
allotted a certain amount of time to sow, plant, and weed and reap. If you sit idly by,
the winds of adversity, trials of life and predators will rule your garden. But if you're
using your allotted time to guard what He has given you, you can rest assured that
your garden will not fall prey to these things. Don't compare your garden to anyone
else's, for that will only open a door for the enemy. The harvest is dependent on the
Master Gardener, for He gives the growth. Even though you might not even see it in
your lifetime, you can know that your labor is not in vain and God will continue to
grow the seeds planted until they come to maturity.

Use most of your time to seek the Lord. Recall the Lord's admonition to me, "Do
not be so consumed with the work that I have given you to do that you are no longer
consumed with Me."

Landscaping

*B*efore landscaping your prayer garden, take an account of who's planted in

your life. Annuals and perennials provide a kaleidoscope of color in different
seasons of your life. Earthly gardeners plant them to blossom in timely manners so
that there is color manifesting all through the year. So it is in the heart; the Master
has planted a variety of people in your life, making life interesting. The "annuals" in

our lives stay for a season, while "perennials" are with us continuously, each requiring different methods of cultivation and seed planting. Be sensitive to the Master's leading.

Pray & Write....

Receive the Harvest

*A*nd now - what you have been waiting for! It's harvest time! Once the fruit is ripe and the harvest is ready, gardeners reap the fruits of their labor. Using the sickle of your faith, you can partake of the harvest. When you receive the fulfillment of God's promise, rejoice and give thanks to the One who is faithful – and reap your reward! Your hard work and tears entitle you to be the first to enjoy the fruits of your labor.

> The hardworking farmer must be first to partake of the crops.
>
> 2 Timothy 2:6 (NKJ)

A Word of Caution

*I*t is exciting when the fruits of your prayers are hanging heavy on the boughs of your life. Yet this would be an easy time to let up on our intercessions.

I was rejoicing at the appearance of fruit in my life. "Finally I can relax," I thought. But then the Lord caught my attention as He spoke this to my heart.

> The boughs of your life are heavy laden with fruit you have sown for years. The fruit is almost ripe. Continue to pray so the worms of this life do not make way and destroy the fruit. You must not stop praying, pray it through. For when fruit is almost ripe it is vulnerable. It is then that bugs love to eat it. So it is in the spirit world. When the fruit is heavy laden on the bough and almost ripe, the enemy would like to take it for himself and destroy it. Here it is that you must continue to guard it, protect it and keep it from the enemy. The natural tendency would be to pull back, because you see fruit, so you think the answer has come. Don't pull back. It is here that the fruit is most vulnerable. Press in until the fruit is born and even then you must not let up. For when the fruit is picked and in bushel baskets, you must protect it from thieves.

I responded:

Father, thank You for all that You are doing in the lives of those I am praying for. You are faithful! You can do exceeding, abundantly above all that I could ever ask or think according to the power that works within us!

But you, O Lord, are a compassionate and gracious God, slow to anger, abounding in love and faithfulness.   Psalm 86:15

Help me to be faithful in protecting the fruit through prayer, for my prayer and hopes have deep roots in reality. (Phil. 1:7 MSG) Amen.

SOWING SEEDS

*B*e faithful to complete this ministry of prayer that He is calling you to. (Col. 4:17) For when others sense God's presence in your life and the lives of those you're praying for, they too will be drawn to the Master in "The Garden of the Heart."

The seed will grow well, the vine will yield its fruit, the ground will produce its crops, and the heavens will drop their dew. I will give all these things as an inheritance to the remnant of this people.   Zechariah 8:12

_____
_____
_____
_____
_____
_____
_____
_____
_____
_____
_____
_____
_____
_____
_____
Pray and Write !
_____

Garden Checklist

*B*elow you will find bulleted reminders of the cultivation and planting process.

- The best time to cultivate is after the rain. Spend time in the presence of the Holy Spirit, in worship. Wait on Him. Write what He speaks to your heart.

- Cultivate your own heart until it is ready. Is God revealing anything? Write it down in your journal. Respond to God.

- Invite the Holy Spirit to lead you.

- Cultivate the heart of your prodigal by praying:
  o Scriptures on the heart
  o Weed killer scriptures
  o Pray down strongholds
  o Appropriate God's victory over their lives, and Satan's defeat

- Choose scriptures from the different categories and pray them as the Holy Spirit leads you.

- Wait in His presence – write down what God speaks to your heart.

- Record what you see God doing in your prodigals' lives – journal, journal, journal!

Pray & Write....

A Final Word

Enjoy Your Harvest!

> We don't want you in the dark, friends, about how hard it was when all this came down on us in Asia province. It was so bad we didn't think we were going to make it. We felt like we'd been sent to death row, that it was all over for us. As it turned out, it was the best thing that could have happened. Instead of trusting in our own strength or wits to get out of it, we were forced to trust God totally—not a bad idea since he's the God who raises the dead! And he did it, rescued us from certain doom. And he'll do it again, rescuing us as many times as we need rescuing. You and your prayers are part of the rescue operation—I don't want you in the dark about that either. I can see your faces even now, lifted in praise for God's deliverance of us, a rescue in which your prayers played such a crucial part.
>
> 2 Cor. 1:8-11 (MSG)
>
> … "On your knees and pray for **harvest hands**!" Matthew 9:38 (MSG)

Open your hands and get ready for the harvest! "On your knees" speaks of:
- An intimate relationship with God, not a formula.
- A dependence on God, who will lead you into battle.
- Sometimes physically on your knees and sometimes a bended knee reflects an attitude of the heart.

Pray for harvest hands!
- Harvest hands will only be overflowing as God leads you and guides you.
- Each battle is unique and you will have to lean fully on God for direction.
- The weapons you use to win one battle may not be the same weapons that God will lead you to use for another.
- When Joshua failed to ask God's direction in battle, he was deceived by the enemy. (Joshua 9:14, 22) Don't allow yourself to be so deceived – seek God in all things.
- Sometimes God might instruct you to:
  - Pull down strongholds (2 Cor. 10:4-5)
  - Bind or loosen (Matt. 16:19)
  - Pray His Word (Is. 62:6; Is. 55:11)
  - Use praise as a weapon (2 Chron. 20:21, 22)
  - Just stand and watch the salvation of the Lord (2 Chron. 20:17)

- Pray daily for the same situation or pray only once (Luke 18:1-6; Mark 11:24)
- Carry a burden with groans too deep for words (Rom. 8:26-27)
- Overcome evil with good (Rom. 12:21)
- Or fast (Is. 58:6)

> Those who sow tears shall reap joy. Yes, they go out weeping, carrying seed for sowing, and return singing, carrying their sheaves.   Psalm 126:5-6 (TLB)

The Battle is the Lords. (1 Sam. 17:47; 2 Chron. 20:15) Allow Him to lead you into victory!

When King David was a lad, he went out to fight against the giant, Goliath. King Saul outfitted David in armor the same way he outfitted every other soldier going out to battle. But when David was fully dressed, he tried to walk but could hardly budge. So rather than follow someone else's battle plan, he removed the weighted armor, picked up five smooth stones and a slingshot, and went out to meet the giant, Goliath, with the Lord as his only protection.

In the past, David killed a lion and a bear with his bare hands through the strength of his God. David had harvest hands. At times he folded them to pray. At other times, he used a slingshot and a stone or dispelled the enemy by playing anointed music (1 Samuel 16:16-23). But nonetheless, they were harvest hands dedicated to God, and David was reaping what he had sown from his intimacy with God. When David went out to meet Goliath, the giant laughed at little David. David answered:

> "You come at me with sword and spear and battle ax. I come at you in the name of God-of-the-Angel-Armies, the God of Israel's troops, whom you curse and mock. This very day God is handing you over to me. ...The battle belongs to God—he's handing you to us on a platter!"   1 Samuel 17:45-47 (MSG)

David took off from the front line, running toward the Philistine. David reached into his pocket for a stone, slung it, and hit the Philistine hard in the forehead, embedding the stone deeply. The Philistine crashed, face down in the dirt.

The weapons that God calls you to use in battle may not be the same weapons that God led you to use in a previous battle. Be sensitive to the leading of the Holy Spirit. He will show you things to come. (John 16:13)

Recently my son, Joel was on a mission trip. He was heavy on my heart as I fell asleep and I sensed God calling me to pray for him. In the middle of the night I actually saw the word WORSHIP spelled out in a dream. Upon awakening I knew the Lord was directing me to fight this battle through praise and worship as Jehoshaphat did in 2Chron. 20:21, 22.

As they praised, the Lord brought ambushes against their enemies and they were defeated.

Many times when someone is on my heart I begin by praying God's powerful Word into the situation. But this time rather than appropriate all the scriptures on protection, I began to praise God for what He was doing. God was leading me in a specific way in this battle.

Be sensitive to the leading of the Lord for He is the Mighty Warrior who will lead you in battle.

> BLESSED BE the Lord, my Rock and my keen and firm Strength, Who teaches my hands to war and my fingers to fight. Psalm 144:1 (AMP)

On Your Knees and pray for harvest hands!

Father, I offer my hands to You. Give me harvest hands. Train my hands for battle! Thank You for my inheritance - souls! And I:

> ... will come home laughing with armloads of blessings! Psalm 126:6 (MSG)

> ... will not become weary in doing good, for at the proper time I will reap a harvest if I do not give up! Galatians 6:9

Open your hands and praise the Lord of the Harvest. Do not underestimate God! He is faithful who has promised!

> Don't drag your feet. Be like those who stay the course with committed faith and then get everything promised to them. Hebrews 6:12 (MSG)

> So let us seize and hold fast and retain without wavering the hope we cherish and confess and our acknowledgement of it, for He Who promised is reliable (sure) and faithful to His word. Hebrews 10:23 (AMP)

You WILL reap what you sow, praise be to God! May you and your loved ones experience His peace, His abundant joy, His blessings. All power and glory to Him!

Debra

Notes...

Planting Seed

I stayed awake all night, prayerfully pondering your promise.
Psalm 119:148 (MSG)

Scripture Seed

*T*here is nothing more powerful than praying God's Word back to Him. So we've organized the Sword of the Spirit into subjects for you to pray first for those who you're standing in the gap for, and then for yourself as intercessor. May you be encouraged, uplifted and empowered with the Word of God.

> Seize the Word and hold on, no matter what, sticking with it until there's a harvest.   Luke 8:15 (MSG)

*I*f you have yet to establish that relationship with the One who longs for you, you'll find a sample Salvation Prayer on page 201 to begin the most awesome journey you will ever experience. Welcome to the family of God and welcome to the battle lines, dear one.

Seeding the Word

*W*hen you speak the Word of God, it actively carries out God's command, for the Word is living and active, and is full of creative life. When you plant a seed in the ground of the heart, expect it to grow. Do not underestimate God's Word!

"... for whatever a man sows, this he will also reap"   Galatians 6:7 (NASB)

Ten Step Seed Planting Process

1. All scripture seeds will germinate at a higher rate if they are soaked before planting them in the heart. Soak in the presence of the Lord before you plant your seeds and they, too, will grow at a faster rate. Make this a time of worship, confession, repentance and praise. (pgs. 81,82)
2. As a gardener plants a seed in the ground, take a scripture seed and plant it in the soil of the heart. (pgs. 83,84)
3. Now label (write) your prayer request in the "sowing" section of your prayer journal just as you would label seed in an earthly garden. It may take some time before you see it grow. Labeling it will allow you to remember whose heart it was planted in and the type of seed that was planted. (pgs. 84,85)
4. Directly after you plant the seed, you must water it daily, and continue doing so daily by thanking the Lord in faith for doing what He said He would do in His Word. When you see nothing happening with your physical eyes, look through eyes of faith ... eyes that see and believe that God's Word is true when all indications say otherwise. (pgs. 85–87)
5. As you do so, the outer shell of this tiny seed buried secretly in the soil of the heart will open and begin to grow. (pg. 85)
6. As the seed cracks open, the life that is in the seed will begin to spring forth.
7. Tiny roots will form reaching deep in the hidden soil of the heart. (pg. 89)
8. Your seed will begin to sprout upward reaching toward the Light. Be patient here, seeds germinate at different rates. (pg. 91)
9. Eventually, you will see two little green specks peeking out from the soil, reaching toward the Son that will cause them to grow. Once you see the sprouts coming forth, you will need to continue watering through prayer. (pg. 99)
10. In the "reaping" section record the growth you see. This will cause your faith to grow, as you observe God's answers to your prayers. Do not stop praying just because you see the beginning of new growth; for this stage of life is a vulnerable time for your new little seedling. (pg. 99)

Scripture Prayers

♥ Author's Note: Unless otherwise indicated, all scriptures are taken from the Holy Bible, New International Version (NIV)®. Please note these are not direct "quotes," but prayers based on God's precious Word.

Power of God's Word

Praying the following scriptures will build your faith.

Lord, I believe that the Word You speak is alive and full of power [making it active, operative, energizing, and effective]; it is sharper than any two-edged sword, penetrating to the dividing line of the breath of life (soul) and [the immortal] spirit, and of joints and marrow [of the deepest parts of our nature], exposing and sifting and analyzing and judging the very thoughts and purposes of the heart. (Heb. 4:12 AMP)

Jesus, as I abide in You and Your Word abides in me, I can ask whatever I wish and it shall be done unto me, because I am asking for the fulfillment of Your Word. (John 15:7 NASB)

Father, I am so thankful that Jesus Christ—the Living Word—is the same yesterday, today, and forever. (Heb. 13:8)

I choose to speak Your words, Lord, because they are words of life, and my tongue has the power of life and death. (Prov. 18:21)

Father, I stagger not at Your promises through unbelief but I am strong in faith because Your Word is building my faith and making me stronger, and I give You all the glory. Father, I am fully persuaded that what You have promised, You are well able to bring to pass. (Romans 4:20-21 KJV)

Thank You, Jesus, that Your words are spirit and life to _____. (John 6:63)

I bless and praise Your mighty name, Lord, for by Your word the heavens were made, and by the breath of Your mouth all their host. For You spoke, and it was done; You commanded, and it stood fast. (Psalm 33:6, 9 NASB)

Thank You Lord, that You are watching over Your word to perform it. (Jer. 1:12 NASB) I will take with me Your words, and I will present them to You in prayer, Lord. (Hosea 14:2)

Father, You said that Your Word would not come back to You empty or void, but it shall accomplish that which You please and it shall prosper in the things for which You sent it. I pray and speak Your Word over _____'s heart and life. I trust you to perform it and make it come to pass in him/her. (Isaiah 55:11)

I bind Your word continually to _____, and I tie it around her/his neck. When she/he walks about, it will guide her/him; when he/she sleeps, Your word will watch over her/him; and when he/she awakes, it will talk to her/him. (Prov. 6:21-22 NASB)

For Your word is a lamp unto _____'s feet, and a light unto her/his path, for it will show her/him the way he/she should go. (Psalm 119:105)

Thank You Father, that Your Word is life to _____, and healing and health to all her/his flesh. (Prov. 4:22 AMP)

I **SAY** to this mountain of _____, 'Be taken up and cast into the sea,' and I do not doubt in my heart, but believe that what I **SAY i**s going to happen, it shall be granted to me. (Mark 11:23 NASB)

Putting on the Armor of God

Therefore I put on the full armor of God, so that when the day of evil comes, I may be able to stand my ground, and after I have done everything, I will stand. I stand firm then, with the belt of truth buckled around my waist, with the breastplate of righteousness in place, and with my feet fitted with the readiness that comes from the gospel of peace. In addition to all this, I take up the shield of faith, with which I can extinguish all the flaming arrows of the evil one. I take the helmet of salvation and the sword of the Spirit, which is the word of God. And I pray in the Spirit on all occasions with all kinds of prayers and requests. With this in mind, I am alert and always keep on praying for all the saints. (Eph. 6:10-18) I put on the Lord Jesus Christ and make no provision for the flesh. (Romans 13:14)

Heart Scriptures

*A*s you pray these scriptures, the Holy Spirit will soften the stony heart and bring

to the surface any rocks of offense, painful memories, or hard-to-break habits so they can be removed, making it easier for your wayward loved one to yield to the Lord's hand.

Father, open the eyes of _____'s heart and turn her/him from darkness to light, and from the power of Satan unto God, that she/he may receive forgiveness of sins, and an inheritance among them which are sanctified by faith that is in Christ. (Acts 26:18 NASB) Remove the veil that is blinding her/him. (2 Cor. 4:3,4) For I always pray to] the God of our Lord Jesus Christ, the Father of glory, that He may grant _____ a spirit of wisdom and revelation [of insight into mysteries and secrets] in the [deep and intimate] knowledge of Him, by having the eyes of her/his heart flooded with light, so that she/he can know and understand the hope to which He has called her/him, and how rich is His glorious inheritance in the saints (His set-apart ones), (Eph. 1:18 AMP)

Father, You have promised to circumcise my heart and the hearts of my children, which means to open it to the gospel and take away all hindrances in obeying the truth. You will do this so that they will love You with all of their hearts and all of their souls, and live. (Deut. 30:6)

Thank You, Father, that You have promised to give _____ a new heart and put a new spirit within her/him; and that You will take away her/his heart of stone and give her/him a heart of flesh. Thank You for putting Your Spirit within _____ and causing her/him to walk in Your statutes, and to keep Your judgments and do them. (Ezek. 36:26-27 NKJ)

Thank You, Lord for giving _____ a heart to know You, for then she/he will return to You with her/his whole heart. (Jer. 24:7 NASB)

Thank You, Father, for giving _____ one heart and one way, that she/he may fear You forever for her/his good, and the good of her/his children. (Jer. 32:39 NASB)

Father, I lay hold of Your covenant for _____. You said that You have made an everlasting covenant with _____, that You will not turn away from her/him, to do them good; but You will put Your fear in her/his heart so he/she will not depart from You. (Jer. 32:40 KJV)

Teach _____ Your way, O Lord, so she/he will walk in Your truth. Give her/him an undivided heart so she/he will fear Your name. (Ps. 86:11)

You have promised to pour Your Spirit upon my seed and Your blessings upon my offspring. You will pour water upon them and floods upon the dry ground of their hearts because she/he is spiritually thirsty. (Is. 44:3 KJV)

Thank you for guiding _____ in all truth. (John 16:13)

Search _____, O God, and know her/his heart: try her/him, and know her/his thoughts: And see if there be any wicked way in _____, and lead her/him in the way everlasting. (Psalms 139:23, 24 KJV) Purge _____ with hyssop, and she/he shall be whiter than snow. Hide Your face from _____'s sins, and blot out all her/his iniquities. Create in _____ a clean heart, O God; and renew a right spirit within her/him. Cast _____ not away from Your presence; and take not Your Holy Spirit from her/him. Restore unto _____ the joy of Your salvation; and uphold her/him with Your free spirit. (Psalm 51:7, 9-12 KJV)

Strengthen _____'s heart so that she/he will be blameless and holy in the presence of our God and Father when our Lord Jesus comes with all his holy ones. (1 Thess. 3:13)

Father, I loose the love of God that has been shed abroad in _____'s heart. (Rom. 5:5 KJV)

I pray that the spirit of truth would guide _____ into all truth. (John 16:13) Help _____ to hold onto your teaching that she/he shall know the truth, and the truth shall make her/him free. (John 8:32) Teach _____ your way, O LORD, and she/he will walk in Your truth; (Psalm 86:11) Jesus answered, "I am the way and the truth and the life." (John 14:6)

Father, remove unbelief from _____'s heart. Open the door for her/him to hear your word, for faith comes from hearing and hearing by the word of God. (Romans 10:17)

I bind Your word to her/his heart. When she/he walks, they will guide her/him; when she/he sleeps, they will watch over her/him; when she/he awakens, they will speak to her/him. (Prov. 6:21, 22)

Father, I thank You that _____'s heart is in Your hand; turn it like rivers of water towards Your will. (Prov. 21:1 NKJ)

Pulling Down Strongholds

*U*se the powerful weapons God has given you and uproot strongholds through prayer.

The Living Bible says,

These weapons can break down every proud argument against God and every wall that can be built to keep men from finding him. With these weapons I can capture rebels and bring them back to God and change them into men whose hearts' desire is obedience to Christ. (2 Cor. 10:4-5)

1. Listen to the Holy Spirit. He can reveal strongholds to your heart, for He alone knows the hearts of all men. (1 Kings 8:39)
2. God has also given us a window into their hearts. From the heart, the mouth speaks. Pay attention to what comes out of their mouth. (Luke 6:45)

In Jesus' name, I pull down and destroy every stronghold, imagination, argument and high thing that raises itself against the knowledge of God's word in _____'s heart. I pull down the stronghold(s) of pride, unbelief, false theologies, deception and _____. Father take _____'s thoughts captive to the obedience of Jesus Christ. I bind his/her heart to God's word of truth. When he/she walks about, it will guide him/her. When he/she sleeps, it will watch over him/her, and when _____awakens, it will talk to him/her. (2 Cor. 10:4-5 NAS; Prov. 6:21-22)

Additional Examples of Strongholds are:

- Bitterness
- Unforgiveness
- Pride
- Anger
- Lust
- Hate

- Fear
- Condemnation
- Failure
- Jealousy or rejection
- Love of money
- Perversity

Weed-Killer Prayers

*O*nce you have prayed the heart scriptures to soften the soil of the heart, pray these weed-killer scriptures to destroy weeds of sin.

Father, in the name of Jesus I come before You on behalf of _____, and claim Your word that says sin shall no longer have dominion over him/her, and that he/she is dead to sin and his/her relation to it is broken. In faith I proclaim that he/she is alive to You Lord God, living in unbroken fellowship with You in Christ Jesus. Sin shall no longer reign in his/her mortal body so that he/she may obey its lusts. (Rom. 6:11, 12, 14 AMP) I declare that she/he is crucified to this world and this world is crucified to her/him. (Gal. 6:14)

Jesus died for_____ and his/her old self was crucified with Christ in order that his/her body of sin might be done away with, so that _____will no longer be a slave to sin. (Rom. 6:6)

Therefore, I declare the sins of the flesh to be powerless over _____. I loose the following sins from his/her heart: Immorality, impurity, indecency, idolatry, sorcery, enmity, strife, jealousy, anger, (ill-temper), selfishness, divisions, (dissentions) party spirit (factions, sects, peculiar opinions, heresies), envy, drunkenness, carousing and the like. (Gal. 5:19-21)

Alphabetical Prayers

*T*he following Scriptures are listed topically in alphabetical order. Pray these as the Holy Spirit leads you.

Abandonment

"Father I thank You that You will never leave nor forsake _____." (Hebrews 13:5) "You are with _____ always, even to the end of the age." (Matthew 28:20) Though _____ is surrounded by troubles, you will bring her/him safely through them. You will clench your fist against her/his angry enemies! Your power will save her/him. You will work out your plans for _____'s life – for your loving-kindness, Lord, continues forever. Father, thank You for not abandoning _____, for You made her/him. (Ps. 138:7-8 AMP)

Abundant life

The thief does not come except to steal, and to kill, and to destroy. But You, oh Lord, have come that _____ may have life, and that she/he may have it more abundantly. (John 10:10)

Angelic Help

I praise You, Father, that Your angels perform Your word, and they obey the voice of Your word, when I speak Your word.

Bless the LORD, you His angels, Mighty in strength, who perform His word, obeying the voice of His word! (Ps. 103:20 NASB) He will give His angels [especial] charge over _____ to accompany and defend and preserve her/him in all your ways [of obedience and service]. (Ps. 91:11 AMP) Your angels, O Lord, encamp around _____ and rescue _____ because she/he fears You. (Ps. 34:7)

Father, I pray that those who seek _____'s life will be disgraced and put to shame; those who plot _____'s ruin be turned back in dismay. They will be like chaff before the wind, with the angel of the LORD driving them away; their path will be dark and slippery, with the angel of the LORD pursuing them. Since they hid their net for _____ without cause, and without cause dug a pit for _____, ruin shall overtake them by surprise, the net they hid shall entangle them, they shall fall into the pit, to their ruin. (Ps. 35:4-8)

Anxieties

In the multitude of _____'s anxieties within her/him/me, Your comforts delight her/his/my soul. (Psalm 94:19) Help _____ to cast the whole of her/his care [all their anxieties, worries, and concerns, once and for all] on You, Lord, for You care for _____ affectionately and care about her/him watchfully. [Ps. 55:22] (1 Peter 5:7 AMP)

Blindness

Father, remove the veil that is blinding _____. (2 Cor. 3:16-17) Open _____'s eyes and turn her/him from darkness to light, and from the power of Satan unto God, that she/he may receive forgiveness of sins, and an inheritance among them, which are sanctified by faith that is in Christ. (Acts 26:18) Father, remove hate from _____'s heart. For whoever hates his brother is in darkness and walks around in darkness; she/he does not know where she/he is going, because the darkness has blinded her/him. (1 John 2:11)

Blood of the Lamb

I apply the blood of Jesus over _____, for I overcome the enemy by the blood of the Lamb and the word of my testimony. (Rev. 12:11) Where the blood of Jesus is applied the destroyer cannot come in. (Ex. 12:23) Father I appropriate the blood of Jesus for peace in her/his life. (Col. 1:20) I declare that she/he is redeemed through the blood. (Eph. 1:7) In whom we have redemption through his blood, even the forgiveness of sins. (Col. 1:14 KJV)

Just think how much more surely the blood of Christ will transform our lives and hearts. Father, transform _____'s life and heart and cleanse his/her conscience through the blood of Jesus. (Heb. 9:14 TLB) Protect her/him from evil through the blood. (Eph. 1:7) Thank You Lord, she/he has been purchased with the blood. (Acts 20:28) In Jesus Name.

Captivity

I pray that _____ will come to her/his senses and escape from the trap of the devil, who has taken her/him captive to do his will. (2 Tim. 2:26)

You say that even though _____ has become prey to the mighty or has been taken captive lawfully, she/he shall be delivered. For You will contend with those that contend with me, and You will save my children. (Isaiah 49:24-25)

Children

Thank You for Your Word that says, "Refrain your voice from weeping, and your eyes from tears; For your work shall be rewarded, says the Lord, And they shall come back from the land of the enemy. There is hope in your future, says the Lord, that your children shall come back to their own border." (Jer. 31:16, 17 NKJV)

I thank You that Your covenant with them is that Your Spirit, which is upon me, and Your words which You have put in my mouth, shall not depart from my children or from their mouth, or from their descendants' mouth. (Isa. 59:21)

My children shall dwell safely and continue, and their descendants shall be established before You. (Ps. 102:28 AMP) The seed of the righteous shall be delivered. (Prov. 11:21 KJV) Deliver _____ from the snare of the trapper. (Ps. 91:31 NASB) You said in Isaiah 49:24-25 that even though _____ has become prey to the mighty or has been taken captive lawfully, she/he shall be delivered. For You will contend with those that contend with me, and You will save my children.

You have promised to pour Your Spirit upon my seed and Your blessings upon my offspring. (Is. 44:3 KJV) You will pour water upon them and floods upon the dry ground of their hearts because she/he is spiritually thirsty. All my children will be taught of the Lord; And the well-being of my children will be great. (Is. 54:13 NASB)

And You oh Lord, shall turn and reconcile the hearts of the [estranged] fathers to the [ungodly] children, and the hearts of the [rebellious] children to [the piety of] their fathers [a reconciliation produced by repentance of the ungodly... (Mal. 4:6 AMP)

But our families will continue; generation after generation will be preserved by your protection. (Psalm 102:28 TLB)

I will not fear, for You are with me; You will bring my offspring from the east, And gather them from the west. You will say to the north, 'Give them up!' And to the south, 'Do not hold them back.' Bring My sons from afar, and my daughters from the ends of the earth (Isa. 43:5-6 NASB). No one can snatch them out of Your hand (John 10:29). My children will be mighty in the land; the generation of the upright will be blessed. (Ps.112: 2). I believe in the Lord Jesus, and me and my household will be saved. (Acts 16:31)

And they answered, Believe in the Lord Jesus Christ [give yourself up to Him, take yourself out of your own keeping and entrust yourself into His keeping] and you will be saved, [and this applies both to] you and your household as well. (Acts 16:31 AMP)

He will deliver the one who is not innocent, who will be delivered through the cleanness of my hands."(Job 22:30) Praise the LORD. Blessed is the man who fears the LORD, who finds great delight in his commands. (Ps. 112:1)

My children shall dwell safely and continue, and their descendants shall be established before You. (Ps. 102:28 AMP)

Cleansing

Purge _____ with hyssop, and she/he shall be whiter than snow. Hide Your face from _____'s sins, and blot out all her/his iniquities. Create in _____ a clean heart, O God; and renew a right spirit within her/him. Cast _____ not away from Your presence; and take not Your Holy Spirit from her/him. Restore unto _____ the joy of Your salvation; and uphold her/him with Your free spirit. Then will _____ teach transgressors thy ways; and sinners shall be converted unto You. (Ps. 51:7, 9-13 KJV)

Jesus, thank You for sanctifying _____ and cleansing her/him by the washing of water of Your Word, so You can present her/him to Yourself as a glorious church without spot or wrinkle, or any such thing, but holy and blameless. (Eph. 5:26-27 NAS)

Comfort

Father, thank You for turning _____'s mourning to joy, comfort her/him, and make her/him rejoice rather than sorrow. (Jeremiah 31:13 KJV)

Thank You for comforting the downcast and for comforting _____ (2 Corinthians 7:6)

The LORD is close to the brokenhearted and saves those who are crushed in spirit. (Ps. 34:18) Even though _____walks through the valley of the shadow of death, she/he will fear no evil, for you are with her/him; your rod and your staff, they comfort her/him. (Ps. 23:4) The LORD will surely comfort _____and will look with compassion on all her/his ruins; He will make her/his deserts like Eden, her/his wastelands like the garden of the LORD. Joy and gladness will be found in _____, thanksgiving and the sound of singing. (Isa. 51:3) I always strive for _____earnestly in my prayer, [pleading] that she/he may [as persons of ripe character and clear conviction] stand firm and mature [in spiritual growth], convinced and fully assured in everything willed by God. (Col. 4:12 AMP)

Conviction

Thank You Lord that Your Spirit of Truth will come and ... convict _____of sin and righteousness and judgment in her/his life. (John 16:8)

Counsel

Where there is no counsel, the people fall; But in the multitude of counselors there is safety. (Proverbs 11:14 KJV) The Lord brings the counsel of the nations to naught; He makes the thoughts and plans of the peoples of no effect. (Psalm 33:10 AMP)

Thank You Lord for bringing worldly counsel to naught in _____' s life. Uproot thoughts and ideas from her/his heart, that are not of You. Bring godly counsel into her/his life.

Deliverance

Lord, I thank You that You will deliver the one for whom I intercede that is not innocent. Yes, _____will be delivered through the cleanliness of my hands. (Job 22:30)

Many are the afflictions of the righteous; but You LORD deliver _____out of them all. (Ps. 34:19 KJV) The seed of the righteous shall be delivered. (Prov. 11:21 KJV) Deliver _____ from the snare of the trapper. (Ps. 91:3 NASB)

And you can also be very sure God will rescue the children of the godly. (Prov. 11:21 TLB)

Lord, deliver _____ from the way of the evil man, from the man that speaks perverse things, from those who leave the paths of uprightness, to walk in the ways of darkness; Who delight in doing evil, and rejoice in the perversity of evil; Whose paths are crooked, and who are devious in their ways. (Prov. 2:12-15 NASB)

Thank You for Your Word that says, "Refrain your voice from weeping, And your eyes from tears; For your work shall be rewarded, says the Lord, And they shall come back from the land of the enemy. There is hope in your future, says the Lord, that your children shall come back to their own border." (Jer. 31:16-17)

Thank You that You send forth Your Word and healed _____ and rescued her/him/me from the pit and destruction. (Ps. 107:20 AMP)

Thank You for Your word Lord, that says, "Because he loves me," says the LORD, "I will rescue him; I will protect him, for he acknowledges my name. He will call upon me, and I will answer him; I will be with him in trouble, I will deliver him and honor him. (Ps. 91:14-15 NKJ)

You are _____'s hiding place; You shall preserve her/him from trouble; You shall surround her/him with songs of deliverance. Selah (Ps. 32:7 NAS) _____ shall call upon Me, and I will answer him; I will be with him in trouble; I will deliver him and honor him. (Ps. 91:15 NAS) For You have delivered _____'s soul from death, her/his eyes from tears, And her/his feet from falling. (Ps. 116:8 KJV) And the Lord will deliver _____ from every evil attack and preserve her/him for His heavenly kingdom. To Him be glory forever and ever. Amen! (2 Timothy 4:18 AMP) Deliver _____, O LORD, from her/his enemies; _____ hides herself/himself in You. (Ps. 143:9)

The LORD is _____'s rock and her/his fortress and deliverer; her/his God, and strength, in whom _____ will trust; her/his shield and the horn of her/his salvation and her/his stronghold. (Ps. 18:2 AMP)

I thank You Lord that even though _____ has become prey to the evil one and taken captive through her/his sin, Your word says that she/he will be delivered. For You will contend with those who contend with me and you will save my children! (Is. 49:24, 25 NKJ)

He has delivered and drawn us to Himself out of the control and the dominion of darkness and has transferred us into the kingdom of the Son of His love. (Col. 1:13 AMP)

But those who suffer He delivers in their suffering; he speaks to them in their affliction. (Job 36:15). Father, reach down your hand from on high; deliver _____ and rescue her/him from the mighty waters, from the hands of foreigners whose mouths are full of lies, whose right hands are deceitful. (Ps. 144:7-8)

And I will deliver _____ out of the hand of the wicked, and I will redeem _____ out of the hand of the terrible. (Jer. 15:21 KJV)

And they shall fight against you, but they shall not [finally] prevail against you, for I am with you, says the Lord, to deliver you. (Jer. 1:19-2:1 AMP)

Through You we push back our enemies; through Your name we trample our foes. I do not trust in my bow, my sword does not bring me victory; but You give us victory over our enemies, You put our adversaries to shame. In God we make our boast all day long, and we will praise Your name forever. (Ps. 44:5-8)

Depression

The LORD opens the eyes of the blind; The LORD raises those who are bowed down; The LORD loves the righteous. (Psalm 146:8 NAS)

_____shall ARISE [from the depression and prostration in which circumstances have kept her/him—she/he shall rise to a new life]! She/he shall shine (be radiant with the glory of the Lord), for her/his light has come, and the glory of the Lord has risen upon _____! (Is. 60:1 AMP)

Direction

Lord, according to Your word, instruct _____ and teach her/him in the way she/he should go; counsel her/him with Your eye upon her/him. (Ps. 32:8 AMP)

Teach _____ to do Your will, for You are her/his/my God; let Your good Spirit lead her/him/me into a level country and into the land of uprightness. (Ps. 143:10 AMP)

Discipline

Thank You Father that whom You love, You correct, just as a father corrects the son in whom he delights. (Proverbs 3:12 AMP) Because the Lord disciplines those he loves, and he punishes everyone he accepts as a son. (Hebrews 12:6)

Evil Days

Help _____ to walk circumspectly, not as fools but as wise, redeeming the time, because the days are evil. Therefore _____will not be unwise, but understand what the will of the Lord is. (Ephesians 5:15-17 NKJ)

Teach her/him the brevity of life so that she/he may grow in wisdom. (Ps. 90:12 NLT) Teach _____to number her/his days and recognize how few they are; help her/him to spend them as she/he should. (Ps. 90:12 TLB)

Fear

There is no fear in love; but perfect love casts out fear, because fear involves torment. (1 John 4:18 NKJ)

Lord, reveal Your love to _____. For You have not given _____ a spirit of fear, but of power and of love and of a sound mind. (2 Timothy 1:7 KJV)

Cause _____ to seek You and as she/he does, hear her/him and deliver her/him from all her/his fears. (Psalm 34:4 KJV)

[A Psalm of David.] The LORD is _____'s light and salvation; Whom shall she/he fear? The LORD is the strength of her/his life; Of whom shall she/he be afraid? (Psalm 27:1 KJV)

I pray that _____ is strong and courageous, Lord, for Your word says, "Do not be afraid or terrified because of them, for the LORD your God goes with you; he will never leave you nor forsake you." (Deut. 31:6)

For I am the LORD, your God, who takes hold of _____'s right hand and says to her/him, Do not fear; I will help you. (Isa. 41:13)

I say to _____'s fearful heart, "Be strong, do not fear; your God will come, he will come with vengeance; with divine retribution he will come to save you." (Isa. 35:4)

I pray that _____will not be afraid of the enemy, for the LORD my God himself will fight for her/him/me. (Deut. 3:22)

In righteousness _____ will be established; _____ will be far from oppression, for _____ will not fear; and from terror, for it will not come near her/him/me. (Is. 54: 14 NASB)

Forgiveness

If _____ confesses her/his sins, He is faithful and just to forgive her/him of her/his sins and to cleanse him/her from all unrighteousness. (1 John 1:9)

In Him _____ has redemption through His blood, the forgiveness of sins, according to the riches of His grace. (Ephesians 1:7)

Future and Hope

For I know the thoughts that I think toward _____, says the LORD, thoughts of peace and not of evil, to give him/her a future and a hope. Then she/he will call upon Me and go and pray to Me, and I will listen to him/her. And she/he will seek Me and find Me, when she/he searches for Me with all his/her heart. I will be found by_____, says the LORD, and I will bring her/him back from her/his captivity. (Jeremiah 29:11-14)

Help _____ forget those things which are behind and reach forward to those things which are ahead. (Philippians 3:13)

Your beauty and love chase after _____every day of her/his life. She/he is back home in the house of God for the rest of her/his life (Ps. 23:6 MSG). I pray that _____ will not drag her/his feet, but will stay the course with committed faith and then get everything promised to her/him. (Hebrews 6:12 MSG)

I pray that _____won't for a minute envy careless rebels; Draw _____to soak in the Fear-of-God — That's where her/his future lies. Then she/he won't be left with an armload of nothing. (Proverbs 23:17-18 MSG)

Generational Curses

I declare any curse placed upon _____ to be inoperative against her/him in the mighty name of Jesus. I take the authority You have given me and I cancel all Satan's plans and call forth the plans of the Father. For Christ redeemed _____ from the curse of the law and has been made a curse for her/him. (Gal. 3:13) For the law of the Spirit of life in Christ Jesus has set _____ free from the law of sin and death. I break the power of all bondages that have come as a result of the sins of _____or her/his forefathers or relatives. I bind the power of all curses from ever manifesting themselves in _____'s life. I loose the deliverance that Jesus paid for redeeming her/him with His blood (Matt. 18:18), in Jesus Name.

I will give you the keys of the kingdom of heaven; whatever you bind on earth will be bound in heaven, and whatever you loose on earth will be loosed in heaven. (Matt. 16:19)

Grief

You have turned _____'s mourning into dancing; (Psalm 30:11)

Healing

_____ shall not die but live, and will proclaim what the LORD has done. (Psalm 118:17) ... for it is God who works in _____ to will and to act according to his good purpose. (Phil. 2:13) I will hold unswervingly to the hope I profess, for He who promised is faithful. (Hebrews 10:23) Lord cause _____ to pay attention to what You say; and listen closely to Your words. For if she/he will not let them out of her/his sight, and keep them within her/his heart; they will be life and health to her/his whole body. (Proverbs 4:20-23) Satisfy _____ with a long life and show her/him Your salvation. (Psalm 91:16) Lord, bring healing to _____'s body, soul and spirit. I stand in the gap for her/him and decree that she/he is redeemed with the blood of Jesus Christ. (1 Peter 1:18-19) And by Your stripes _____ is healed. (Is 53:5 KJV) You sent forth Your word and healed her/him. You rescued her/him from the grave. (Ps. 107:20) ... You came that she/he may have and enjoy life, and have it in abundance (to the full, till it overflows). (John 10:10 AMP) Lord, You are her/his healer. (Ex. 15:26) Make Yourself known to her/him.

Hearing God

Open _____'s spiritual ears to hear Your voice calling her/him to return to You and receive Your promise to heal her/his backslidings. (Jer. 3:22)

I pray that _____ will trust God from the bottom of her/his heart; and won't try to figure out everything on her/his own. But rather, listen for God's voice in everything she/he does, everywhere she/he goes; For You Lord are the One who will keep her/him on track. Help her/him to not assume that she/he knows it all. Cause her/him to run to You, God and to run from evil! (Proverbs 3:5 MSG)

I bind God's Word upon _____'s heart forever; and fasten them around her/his neck. When she/he walks, they will guide her/him; when she/he sleeps, they will watch over her/him; when she/he awakes, they will speak to her/him. (Prov. 6:21-22)

You [the Lord] will instruct _____ and teach her/him in the way she/he should go; You will counsel her/him with Your eye upon her/him. (Ps. 32:8 AMP)

Hiding Place/Shield

You are _____'s hiding place and shield; (Psalm 119:114) Cause her/him to dwell in the secret place of the Most High so that she/he shall abide under the shadow of the Almighty. (Psalm 91:1)

Holiness

I pray that _____ will come out from (the world), and be separate and touch not the unclean thing so that You will receive her/him back. (2 Cor. 6:17)

Holy Spirit

I thank You that Your covenant with them is that Your Spirit which is upon me and Your words which You have put in my mouth shall not depart from me or from my children's mouth or from their offspring's mouth from this time or forever. (Is. 59:21)

For You will pour water on the thirsty land, and streams on the dry ground; You will pour out Your Spirit on my offspring, and Your blessing on my descendants. They will spring up like grass in a meadow, like poplar trees by flowing streams. One will say, 'I belong to the LORD;' another will call himself by the name of Jacob; still another will write on his hand, 'The LORD's,' and will take the name Israel. (Is. 44:3-5)

So [as the result of the Messiah's intervention] _____ shall [reverently] fear the name of the Lord from the west, and His glory from the rising of the sun. When the enemy shall come in like a flood, the Spirit of the Lord will lift up a standard against him and put him to flight [for He will come like a rushing stream which the breath of the Lord drives]. [Matt. 8:11; Luke 13:29] (Isa. 59:19 AMP)

Love

For I am persuaded that neither death nor life, nor angels nor principalities nor powers, nor things present nor things to come, nor height nor depth, nor any other created thing, shall be able to separate _____ from the love of God which is in Christ Jesus our Lord. (Romans 8:38-39)

Who is he who condemns? It is Christ who died, and furthermore is also risen, who is even at the right hand of God, who also makes intercession for us. Who shall separate us from the love of Christ? Shall tribulation, or distress, or persecution, or famine, or nakedness, or peril, or sword? (Romans 8:34-35 NKJ)

The LORD has appeared of old to _____, saying, "Yes, I have loved you with an everlasting love; Therefore with loving kindness I have drawn you." (Jeremiah 31:3 NKJ)

For God so loved the world that He gave His only begotten Son, _____ believes in Him and shall not perish but have everlasting life. (John 3:16 NAS)

Now hope does not disappoint, because the love of God has been poured out in _____'s heart by the Holy Spirit who was given to her/him. (Romans 5:5)

But God demonstrates His own love toward us, in that while _____ was still a sinner, Christ died for her/him. (Romans 5:8 NKJ)

Father, cause _____ to love the LORD her/his God with all her/his heart, with all her/his soul, and with all her/his mind. (Matthew 22:37)

By this shall _____ know love, because He laid down His life for her/him. (1 John 3:16)

In this is love, not that we loved God, but that He loved us and sent His Son to be the propitiation for our sins. (1 John 4:10)

The love of God has been shed abroad in _____'s heart by the Holy Ghost. (Romans 5:5)

For God did not give _____ a spirit of timidity, but a spirit of power, of love and of self-discipline. (2 Tim. 1:7)

Peace

Father You said, "Peace I leave with _____; my peace I give her/him." You do not give to _____ as the world gives. Cause her/his heart not to be troubled and not to be afraid. (John 14:27)

All my sons will be taught by the LORD, and great will be my children's peace. (Isa. 54:13)

I lift up my eyes to the hills – where does my help come from? My help comes from the LORD, the Maker of heaven and earth. He will not let _____'s foot slip – he who watches over her/him will not slumber; indeed, he who watches over Israel will neither slumber nor sleep. The LORD watches over _____ – the LORD is her/his shade at your right hand; the sun will not harm her/him by day, nor the moon by night. The LORD will keep her/him from all harm – he will watch over her/his life; the LORD will watch over her/his coming and going both now and forevermore. (Ps. 121:1-8) The LORD is a refuge for the oppressed, a stronghold in times of trouble. (Ps. 9:9)

Protection

Can plunder be retrieved from a giant, prisoners of war gotten back from a tyrant? But God says, "Even if a giant grips the plunder and a tyrant holds my people prisoner, I'm the one who's on your side, defending your cause, rescuing your children. And your enemies, crazed and desperate, will turn on themselves, killing each other in a frenzy of self-destruction. Then everyone will know that I, God, have saved you—I, the Mighty One of Jacob." (Isa. 49:24-25 MSG)

The Lord is faithful, and he will strengthen and protect _____ from the evil one. (2 Thess. 3:3)

No one is able to snatch _____ out of Your hand. (John 10:29)

The eternal God is _____'s refuge, and underneath are the everlasting arms. He will drive out _____'s enemy before her/him/me, saying, 'Destroy him!' (Deut. 33:27)

_____ will call on God, and the LORD will rescue her/him. Morning, noon, and night _____ pleads aloud in her/his distress, and the LORD hears her/his voice. He rescues her/him and keeps her/him safe from the battle waged against her/him, even though many still oppose her/him. (Ps. 55:16-18 NLT)

Shall the prey be taken from the mighty, or the lawful captives of the just be delivered? For thus says the Lord: Even the captives of the mighty will be taken away, and the prey of the terrible will be delivered; for I will contend with him who contends with you, and I will give safety to your children and ease them. (Isa. 49:24-25 AMP)

Lord, thank you for Your word that says when _____ passes through the waters, You will be with her/him; and when she/he passes through the rivers, they will not sweep over her/him. When _____ walks through the fire, she/he will not be burned; the flames will not set her/him ablaze. (Isa. 43:2)

My Redeemer is strong; the LORD Almighty is His name. He will vigorously defend _____'s cause so that He may bring rest to her/his/my land. (Jer. 50:34)

Because _____ dwells in the shelter of the Most High, he/she will rest in the shadow of the Almighty. _____ will say of the LORD, "He is my refuge and my fortress, my God, in whom I trust." Surely He will save _____ from the fowler's snare and from the deadly pestilence. He will cover _____ with His feathers, and under His wings _____ will find refuge; His faithfulness will be _____'s shield and rampart. _____ will not fear the terror of night, nor the arrow that flies by day, nor the pestilence that stalks in the darkness, nor the plague that destroys at midday. A thousand may fall at _____'s side, ten thousand at your right hand, but it will not come near _____. (Ps. 91:1-7)

No weapon formed against _____ shall prosper, and every tongue which rises against _____ in judgment You shall condemn. This is the heritage of the servants of the LORD, and their righteousness is from Me, says the LORD. (Isa. 54:17 NAS)

Thank You Lord that when the enemy comes in like a flood, the Spirit of the LORD will lift up a standard against him. (Isa. 59:19 KJV)

Protection from Evil Men

No one is able to snatch _____ out of Your hand. (John 10:29)

I, even I, am He who comforts you. Who are you that you should be afraid of a man who will die, And of the son of a man who will be made like grass? (Isaiah 51:12)

You shall hide _____ in the secret place of Your presence from the plots of man; You shall keep _____ secretly in a pavilion from the strife of tongues. (Ps. 31:20 NKJ)

Fill _____ with wisdom, discretion and understanding so that he/she will be delivered from the way of the evil man, from the man that speaks perverse things, from those who leave the paths of uprightness, to walk in the ways of darkness; Who delight in doing evil, and rejoice in the perversity of evil; Whose paths are crooked, and who are devious in their ways. (Prov. 2:10-15 NAS)

Thank You, Lord that You will deliver _____ from the hand of the wicked, and redeem _____ from the grasp of the violent. (Jer. 15:21)

I pray that _____ will be delivered from wicked and evil men, for not everyone has faith. Lord, You are faithful, and will strengthen and protect _____ from the evil one. (2 Thess. 3:2-3 NASB)

"I am with you to rescue and save _____," declares the LORD. "I will save _____ from the hands of the wicked and redeem her/him from the grasp of the cruel." (Jer. 15:20-21 NAS)

In God I trust; I will not be afraid. What can man do to me? (Ps. 56:11)

_____ dwells in the shelter of the Most High and will rest in the shadow of the Almighty. She/he will say of the LORD, "He is my refuge and my fortress, my

God, in whom I trust." Surely He will save _____ from the fowler's snare and from the deadly pestilence. He will cover her/him with his feathers, and under His wings she/he will find refuge; His faithfulness will be her/his shield and rampart. _____ will not fear the terror of night, nor the arrow that flies by day, nor the pestilence that stalks in the darkness, nor the plague that destroys at midday. A thousand may fall at _____'s side, ten thousand at her/his right hand, but it will not come near _____. She/he will only observe with her/his eyes and see the punishment of the wicked. If _____ makes the Most High her/his dwelling--even the LORD, who is my refuge – then no harm will befall her/him, no disaster will come near her/his tent. For He will command His angels concerning _____ to guard her/him in all her/his ways; they will lift _____ up in their hands, so that she/he will not strike her/his foot against a stone. _____ will tread upon the lion and the cobra; _____ will trample the great lion and the serpent. "Because he loves me," says the LORD, "I will rescue him; I will protect him, for he acknowledges my name. He will call upon me, and I will answer him; I will be with him in trouble, I will deliver him and honor him. With long life will I satisfy him and show him my salvation." (Ps. 91:1-16)

The Lord also will be a refuge and a high tower for the oppressed, a refuge and a stronghold in times of trouble (high cost, destitution, and desperation). (Ps. 9:9 AMP)

Provision

Now to Him who is able to do exceedingly abundantly above all that we ask or think, according to the power that works in us. (Eph. 3:20)

But those who desire to be rich fall into temptation and a snare, and into many foolish and harmful lusts which drown men in destruction and perdition. For the love of money is a root of all kinds of evil, for which some have strayed from the faith in their greediness, and pierced themselves through with many sorrows. But you, O man of God, flee these things and pursue righteousness, godliness, faith, love, patience, gentleness. (1 Timothy 6:9-11 NKJ) Father protect _____ from the love of money. Give _____ a heart to pursue righteousness, godliness, faith, love, patience and gentleness.

He who did not spare His own Son, but delivered Him up for us all, how shall He not with Him also freely give us all things? (Rom. 8:32 NAS) But my God shall supply all _____ needs according to his riches in glory by Christ Jesus. (Phil. 4:19 KJV)

But as it is written, "Eye has not seen, nor ear heard, nor have entered into the heart of man the things which God has prepared for those who love Him." (1 Corinthians 2:9 NKJ)

Purpose

Many are the plans in _____'s mind, but it is Your purpose that will stand for them. (Prov. 19:21) I am confident that You who began a good work in _____ will carry it to completion until the day of Christ Jesus. (Phil. 1:6)

Fill _____ with the full (deep and clear) knowledge of Your will in all spiritual wisdom [in comprehensive insight into the ways and purposes of God] and in understanding and discernment of spiritual things -- That she/he may walk (live and conduct her/him self) in a manner worthy of the Lord, fully pleasing to Him and desiring to please Him in all things, bearing fruit in every good work and steadily growing and increasing in and by the knowledge of God [with fuller, deeper, and clearer insight, acquaintance, and recognition]. [I pray] that she/he will be invigorated and strengthened with all power according to the might of His glory, [to exercise] every kind of endurance and patience (perseverance and forbearance) with joy, Giving thanks to the Father, Who has qualified and made us fit to share the portion which is the inheritance of the saints (God's holy people) in the Light. [The Father] has delivered and drawn _____ to Himself out of the control and the dominion of darkness and has transferred her/him into the kingdom of the Son of His love. (Col. 1:9-13 AMP)

Father cause _____ to roll her/his works upon the Lord [commit and trust them wholly to You; for then You will cause her/his thoughts to become agreeable to Your will, and] so shall their plans be established and succeed. (Prov. 16:3 AMP) Cause her/him to commit her/his way to You, Lord [roll and repose each care of her/his load on You]; trust (lean on, rely on, and be confident) also in You and You will bring it to pass. (Ps. 37:5 AMP)

Rebellion

Lord, please remove the rebellion and worldliness from _____'s heart. Have mercy upon her/him, O God, according to thy lovingkindness: according unto the multitude of thy tender mercies blot out her/his transgressions. Wash _____ thoroughly from her/his iniquity, and cleanse her/him from her/his sin. Bring _____ to acknowledge her/his transgressions: and the sin that is ever before her/him. Against thee, thee only, has _____ sinned, and done this evil in Your sight. (Ps. 51:1-4)

Purge _____ with hyssop, and she/he shall be whiter than snow. Hide Your face from _____'s sins, and blot out all her/his iniquities. Create in _____ a clean heart, O God; and renew a right spirit within her/him. Cast _____ not away from Your presence; and take not Your Holy Spirit from her/him. Restore unto _____ the joy of Your salvation; and uphold her/him with Your free spirit. Then will _____teach transgressors Thy ways; and sinners shall be converted unto You. (Ps. 51:7, 9-13 KJV)

I pray that _____will come out from (the world), and be separate and touch not the unclean thing so that You will receive her/him back. (2 Cor. 6:17)

Thank You for Your Word that says, "Refrain your voice from weeping, And your eyes from tears; For your work shall be rewarded, says the Lord, And they shall come back from the land of the enemy. There is hope in your future, says the Lord, That your children shall come back to their own border." (Jer. 31:16, 17 NKJ)

No temptation has seized _____except what is common to man. And God is faithful; he will not let her/him be tempted beyond what she/he can bear. But when she/he is tempted, He will also provide a way out so that she/he can stand up under it. (1 Cor. 10:13) Therefore, if _____ is in Christ, she/he is a new creation; old things have passed away; behold, all things have become new. (2 Cor. 5:17-18 NKJV) Father, remove any evil companionships from her/his life. Help _____ not to be so deceived and misled! Evil companionships (communion, associations) corrupt and deprave good manners and morals and character. (1 Cor. 15:33 AMP) Father, send forth laborers into Your harvest. (Luke 10:2 KJV)

Repentance

Grant _____repentance so that she/he would confess her/his sins, for I know You will be faithful and just to forgive _____'s sins, and to cleanse her/him from all unrighteousness. (I Jn. 1:9)

Bring _____to the place where she/he will confess her/his faults one to another, and pray one for another, that _____may be healed. (James 5:16)

Alert _____ to know the time, that now it is high time for her/him to awake out of sleep: for now is her/his salvation nearer than when she/he believed. The night is far spent, the day is at hand. I pray that _____will walk honestly, as in the day: not in rioting and drunkenness, not in chambering and wantonness, not in strife and envying. But I pray that _____will put on the Lord Jesus Christ and make no provision for the flesh, to fulfill the lusts thereof. (Rom. 13:11-14 KJV)

O LORD, God of heaven, the great and awesome God, who keeps his covenant of love with those who love him and obey his commands, let your ear be attentive and your eyes open to hear the prayer your servant is praying before you day and night for your servants, the people of Israel. I confess the sins of _____, including myself and my father's house, have committed against you. We have acted very wickedly toward you. We have not obeyed the commands, decrees and laws you gave your servant Moses. Remember the instruction You gave Your servant Moses, saying, "If you are unfaithful, I will scatter you among the nations, but if you return to Me and obey My commands, then even if your exiled people are at the farthest horizon, I will gather them from there and bring them to the place I have chosen as a dwelling for My Name." They are Your servants and Your people, whom You redeemed by Your great strength and Your mighty hand. O Lord, let Your ear be attentive to the prayer of this Your servant and to the prayer of Your servants who delight in revering Your name. (Neh. 1:5-11)

Lord, please remove the rebellion and worldliness from _____'s heart. Have mercy upon her/him, O God, according to Thy loving kindness: according unto the multitude of Thy tender mercies blot out her/his transgressions. Wash _____ thoroughly from her/his iniquity, and cleanse her/him from her/his sin. Bring _____ to acknowledge her/his transgressions, and the sin that is ever before her/him. Against Thee, Thee only, has _____ sinned, and done this evil in Your sight. (Ps. 51:1-4)

I will seek what was lost and bring back what was driven away, bind up the broken and strengthen what was sick. (Ezekiel 34:16 NKJV)

Salvation

The concepts within this manual can also be used to pray for the lost, those who have never come to salvation. Below you will find a scriptural prayer focusing on someone who has never come to the saving knowledge of Christ.

Father, thank you for giving me _____ as my inheritance. (Psalm 2:8) _____ has been translated from the kingdom of darkness into the kingdom of Your Son, Jesus Christ. (Col. 1:13 KJV)

Thank You Lord that You are able to save _____ completely. Cause her/him to come to God through You, because You always live to intercede for her/him. (Heb. 7:25)

I am so thankful, Father, that You love my loved ones so much that You gave Your only begotten Son, Jesus, that if they believe in Him they will not perish, but will have everlasting life. (John 3:16)

For Your hand is not so short that it cannot save, and neither is Your ear so dull that it cannot hear, for whoever calls upon the Name of the Lord shall be saved. (Isaiah 59:1; Acts 2:21)

Thank You, Lord, that You are patient towards _____ and not willing for her/him to perish, but for her/him to come to repentance. (2 Peter 3:9 NKJV)

I lift _____ up to You now, Lord, for Your word says that You will even deliver the one for whom I intercede who is not innocent; yes, he/she will be delivered through the cleanness of my hands. (Job 22:30)

I claim _____ as God's purchased possession, redeemed and loosed by the blood of Christ, and I present them/him/her to You, Father God, in the name of the Lord Jesus Christ. (1 Peter 1:18-19)

My heart's desire and my prayer to You is for their/her/his salvation. (Rom. 10:1)

Therefore, in the name of Jesus Christ, my Lord and Savior, I come boldly before Your throne of grace to obtain mercy and find grace to help on behalf of these who need You. (Heb. 4:16)

O Lord, give them an undivided heart and put a new spirit within them; remove from them their heart of stone and give them a heart of flesh. (Ezekiel 11:19)

Give them a heart to know You, that You are the Lord. For then they will be Your people and You will be their God. (Jer. 24:7)

I pray that today they will hear Your voice and will not harden their hearts with the deceitfulness of sin and unbelief. (Heb. 4:7; 3:13,19)

Plow up the hard ground of their heart and bring repentance so it will be softened to receive the imperishable seed—the living and abiding Word of God. For now is the time for them to seek You, Lord, that You may come and shower salvation upon them. (Hosea 10:12; 1 Peter 1:23)

Grant them repentance that leads to life and to the knowledge of the truth so they may believe the gospel, and receive forgiveness of their sins. (2 Tim. 2:25; Mark 1:15; Luke 24:47)

Cause them to repent so they may be rescued out of the darkness of Satan's kingdom and be brought into the kingdom of your beloved Son, who bought their freedom with His blood and forgave them all their sins. (Col. 1:13-14 NLT)

I pray they will seek You, Lord, while You may be found, that they'll call upon You while You are near, and they will forsake their wicked ways and thoughts, and turn to You. For then You will have compassion on them and will abundantly pardon them. (Is. 55:6-7 KJV)

Father, when they hear the good news of the gospel preached, I pray they will mix it with faith in their hearts so it will benefit them. (Heb. 4:2)

In Jesus' name, I declare that Satan — the one who has blinded the minds of unbelievers — is a defeated foe, because Jesus disarmed him and took away his power, and triumphed over him at the cross. (2 Cor. 4:4; Col. 2:15)

Therefore, I ask the Lord of the harvest to send workers into the harvest field of their hearts to open their blinded eyes, and turn them from darkness to light, and from the power of Satan to God, so they may receive forgiveness for their sins. (Matt. 9:38; Acts 26:18)

When they hear the Gospel preached, remove the veil of unbelief from their hearts, and flood the light of Christ in their hearts so they may see and turn to Him. (2 Cor. 3:15; 4:4)

Grant them a spirit of wisdom and revelation in the knowledge of Christ. I pray that the eyes of their heart may be enlightened so they may know the hope to which You have called them, the riches of Your glorious inheritance in the saints, and Your incomparably great power for us who believe. (Eph. 1:18-19)

I pray they may be found in Christ Jesus, not having a righteousness of their own derived from the law, but may they have a righteousness on the basis of faith in Christ, so they may know Him. (Phil. 3:9)

Father, I pray they will confess with their mouth Jesus as Lord, and believe in their heart that You raised Him from the dead, for then they shall be saved; for with the heart man believes, resulting in righteousness, and with the mouth he confesses, resulting in salvation. (Rom. 10:9-10)

Give them understanding that there is salvation in no one else! Under all heaven there is no other name for people to call upon to save them. (Acts 4:12) Because Jesus is the only Way, the Truth, and the Life, and no one can come to You, Father, except through Him. (John 14:6)

In the name of Jesus, I exercise the power given to me over all the power of the enemy, and I declare every spirit of rebellion, unbelief, pride and deception that is holding my loved ones captive to sin bound. And I loose upon them a spirit of submission, faith, humility and truth so they may know the truth, for the truth will set them free from Satan's power. (Luke 10:19; Matt. 18:18; John 8:32)

I plead the blood of Jesus over them to deliver and cleanse them from their sin, for without the shedding of blood, there is no forgiveness of sin. (Heb. 9:22)

Father, I ask You to open a door for my message, so that I may proclaim the mystery of Christ clearly as I should, and that I will not be ashamed of the gospel of Christ, for it is the power of God for salvation to everyone who believes. (Col. 4:3-4; Rom. 1:16)

I commit them now to Jesus, my Lord and Savior, for He is able to save forever those who draw near to God through Him, since He always lives to make intercession for them. In the name of Jesus I pray. Amen. (Heb. 7:25 NAS)

For God so loved the world that He gave His only begotten Son, that whoever believes in Him should not perish but have everlasting life. (John 3:16)

Because I believe in the Lord Jesus Christ, I declare that I and my household are saved! (Acts 16:31)

Father, open a door for our message, so that we may proclaim the mystery of Christ ... I pray that I may proclaim it clearly, as I should and that I am wise in the way I act toward outsiders; making the most of every opportunity. May my conversation be always full of grace, seasoned with salt, so that I may know how to answer everyone. (Col. 4:2-6)

No one is able to come to You Lord unless the Father Who sent You attracts and draws him and gives him the desire to come to You, and [then] You will raise him up [from the dead] at the last day. (John 6:44 AMP)

Jesus answered, "I am the way and the truth and the life. No one comes to the Father except through me. If you really knew me, you would know my Father as well. From now on, you do know him and have seen him." (John 14:6-7)

The Lord is not slow in keeping his promise, as some understand slowness. He is patient with you, not wanting anyone to perish, but everyone to come to repentance. (2 Peter 3:9)

The Lord does not delay and is not tardy or slow about what He promises, according to some people's conception of slowness, but He is long-suffering (extraordinarily patient) toward you, not desiring that any should perish, but that all should turn to repentance. (2 Peter 3:9 AMP)

Sleep

_____ will both lie down in peace, and sleep; For You alone, O LORD, make her/him dwell in safety. (Psalm 4:8)

_____ lays down and sleeps; and wakens again, for the Lord sustains her/him. _____ will not be afraid of ten thousands of people who have set themselves against her/him round about. Arise, O Lord; save her/him, O my God! For You have struck all her/his enemies on the cheek; You have broken the teeth of the ungodly. Salvation belongs to the Lord; May Your blessing be upon Your people. Selah [pause, and calmly think of that]! (Ps. 3:5-8 AMP)

For you will not go out with haste, nor will you go in flight [as was necessary when Israel left Egypt]; for the Lord will go before you, and the God of Israel will be your rear guard. (Isa. 52:12 AMP)

The Lord shall cause your enemies who rise up against you to be defeated before your face; they shall come out against you one way and flee before you seven ways. (Deut. 28:7 AMP)

Shield

As for God, His way is perfect; the word of the LORD is proven; He is a shield to all who trust in Him. (2 Sam. 22:31) Cause _____ to put her/his trust in you.

Spouse

For this reason a man will leave his father and mother and be united to his wife, and the two will become one flesh. Father, thank you that my spouse and I are one flesh and that my unbelieving spouse has been sanctified through my faith in Christ. (Matt. 19:5)

For the unbelieving husband has been sanctified through his wife, and the unbelieving wife has been sanctified through her believing husband. (1Cor. 7:14)

Strength

But may the God of all grace, who called us to His eternal glory by Christ Jesus, after _____ has suffered a while, perfect, establish, strengthen, and settle her/him. (1 Peter 5:10)

The LORD is _____'s rock and her/his fortress and deliverer; her/his God, strength, in whom _____ will trust; her/his shield and the horn of her/his salvation, her/his stronghold. (Psalm 18:2 NKJV)

_____ can do all things through Christ who strengthens him/her. (Phil. 4:13 NAS)

Your words have upheld _____who was stumbling, and you have strengthened his/her feeble knees; (Job 4:4 NKJ)

Let the words of _____'s mouth and the meditation of her/his heart be acceptable in Your sight, O LORD, her/his strength and Redeemer. (Psalm 19:14)

[We pray] that _____ is invigorated and strengthened with all power according to the might of His glory, [to exercise] every kind of endurance and patience (perseverance and forbearance) with joy. (Col. 1:11 AMP)

Surrender

Bring _____ to the place where she/he will confess her/his faults one to another, and pray one for another, that _____ may be healed. (James 5:16)

Alert _____ to know the time, that now it is high time for her/him to awake out of sleep: for now is her/his salvation nearer than when she/he first believed. The night is far spent, the day is at hand: I pray that _____ will walk honestly, as in the day: not in rioting and drunkenness, not in chambering and wantonness (pleasure mindedness), not in strife and envying. But I pray that _____ will put on the Lord Jesus Christ and make no provision for the flesh, to fulfill the lusts thereof. (Rom. 13:11-14 NKJ)

Temptation

For no temptation (no trial regarded as enticing to sin), [no matter how it comes or where it leads] has overtaken _____ and laid hold on her/him that is not common to man [that is, no temptation or trial has come to _____ that is beyond human resistance and that is not adjusted and adapted and belonging to human experience, and such as man can bear]. But God is faithful [to His Word and to His compassionate nature], and He [can be trusted] not to let _____ be tempted and tried and assayed beyond her/his ability and strength of resistance and power to endure, but with the temptation He will [always] also provide the way out (the means of escape to a landing place), that _____ may be capable and strong and powerful to bear up under it patiently. (1 Cor. 10:13 AMP)

And forgive us our sins, for we also forgive everyone who is indebted to us. And do not lead us into temptation, but deliver us from the evil one. (Luke 11:4)

Thorns

Father, Your Word says that thorns and snares are in the way of the obstinate. Open _____'s eyes to discern why he/she is experiencing the thorns and snares of life.

Thorns and snares are in the way of the obstinate and willful; he who guards himself will be far from them. (Prov. 22:5 AMP)

Truth

And _____ shall know the truth, and the truth shall make her/him free. (John 8:32) Teach _____ your way, O LORD, and she/he will walk in your truth; (Psalm 86:11) I pray that the spirit of truth would penetrate _____'s heart and guide her/him into all truth. (John 16:13) Jesus answered, "I am the way and the truth and the life." (John 14:6)

Wayward Spouse

Scripture prayers for a wayward spouse:

Father, I plead the blood of Jesus over my marriage for reconciliation to You. (2 Cor. 5:18)

I lift up my spouse to the Throne of Grace to receive mercy and grace for help in this time of need. (Heb. 4:16) Turn my spouse's heart like rivers of water toward Your will. (Pr. 21:1 KJV) Remove the veil from her/his eyes. Grant her/him repentance leading to the knowledge of the truth. (1 Tim. 2:4)

In Jesus' Name and by the power of His blood I declare that the enemy is a defeated foe according to Your Word. (Col. 2:15) For Jesus came to destroy the works of the devil (1 John 3:8) and to open my spouse's blinded eyes to make her/him see, to open prison doors to set the captive free. (Luke 4:18) I pray she/he will come to the knowledge of the truth (1 Tim. 2:4), for Your Word says that when she/he knows the truth, the truth will set her/him free, and he who the Son sets free, is free indeed! (John 8:36)

I present my spouse to You Father as a purchased possession by the blood of Jesus, and I plead the blood of Jesus over her/him and appropriate her/his deliverance. (1 Peter 1:18, 19) For we overcome the enemy by the blood of the Lamb and by the word of our testimony. (Rev. 12:11)

Open her/his heart to respond to You, and remove the veil from her/his eyes that is keeping her/him in darkness. Turn her/him from darkness to light, from the power of Satan unto God, so she/he may receive forgiveness of her/his sins. (Acts 26:18) Turn her/his heart to You in repentance for whenever a person turns [in repentance] to the Lord, the veil is stripped off and taken away. Cause her/him to continue to behold [in the Word of God] as in a mirror the glory of the Lord so that she/he will be transfigured into Your very own image in ever increasing splendor and from one degree of glory to another; [for this comes] from the Lord [Who is] the Spirit. (2 Cor. 3:16-18 AMP)

Father, fill my spouse with the Spirit of truth and revelation knowledge. (John 16:13) Give her/him a spirit of wisdom and revelation in the knowledge of You. Enlighten the eyes of her/his heart to know You and the hope of Your calling, and the riches of Your glorious inheritance in the saints. (Eph. 1:17, 18) And now [brethren], I commit _____ to You, God [I deposit her/him in God's charge, entrusting her/him to His protection and care]. And I commend her/him to the Word of His grace [to the commands and counsels and promises of His unmerited favor]. It is able to build her/him up and to give her/him [her/his rightful] inheritance among all God's set-apart ones (those consecrated, purified, and transformed of soul). (Acts 20:32 AMP)

Strengthen me to stand fast. I cast my burden upon You, because You care for me. (1Peter 5:7) Fill me with Your peace and Your hope. With You all things are possible. Nothing is too difficult for You! (Luke 18:26-27; Luke 1:37) Speak clearly to my heart about this situation.

Help me to continue to stand firm for the healing of my marriage, for we are one flesh, and what God has joined together, no man can separate. (Matt. 19:6-7) Because in Your eyes the two of us have become one flesh, I declare victory Lord Jesus, because You prayed to Your Father in John 17:22-23 that we may be one, just as You and the Father are one, that we may be perfected in unity. Therefore I can pray for my spouse with the same authority that I pray for myself.

I declare Your word that says that the separator (the devil) is a defeated foe. You have spoken it, and not one word has failed of all Your good promises, which You promised (1 Kings 8:56). I pray and confess these things in the precious name of Jesus. Amen

Wisdom

If _____ lacks wisdom, I pray that she/he would ask of God, who gives to all liberally and without reproach, and it will be given to her/him. (James 1:5 NAS) For wisdom is better than rubies, and all the things one may desire cannot be compared with her. (Prov. 8:11) So teach _____ to number her/his days, that she/he may gain a heart of wisdom. (Psalm 90:12) When wisdom enters _____'s heart, and knowledge is pleasant to her/his soul, discretion will preserve her/him; understanding will keep her/him. (Prov. 2:9-11) The fear of the LORD is the beginning of wisdom. (Prov. 9:10) Thank you Lord, for putting the fear of God into _____'s heart. (Jer. 32:40 NAS) Help _____ to walk circumspectly, not as fools but as wise, redeeming the time, because the days are evil. Therefore _____ will not be unwise, but understand what the will of the Lord is. (Eph. 5:15 NKJ)

For this reason we also, from the day we heard of it, have not ceased to pray and make [special] request for _____, [asking] that she/he may be filled with the full (deep and clear) knowledge of His will in all spiritual wisdom [in comprehensive insight into the ways and purposes of God] and in understanding and discernment of spiritual things – that she/he may walk (live and conduct him/herself) in a manner worthy of the Lord, fully pleasing to Him and desiring to please Him in all things, bearing fruit in every good work and steadily growing and increasing in and by the knowledge of God [with fuller, deeper, and clearer insight, acquaintance, and recognition]. (Col. 1:9-10 AMP)

But _____ has the mind of Christ (the Messiah) and holds the thoughts (feelings and purposes) of His heart. [Isa. 40:13.] (1 Cor. 2:16 AMP)

Intercessors Section

*I*f God has given you a burden to step in the gap and intercede for someone, embrace this ministry as a gift from the One who gave it.

So he said he would destroy them – had not Moses, his chosen one, stood in the breach before him to keep his wrath from destroying them.   Ps. 106:23

I looked for a man among them who would build up the wall and stand before me in the gap on behalf of the land so I would not have to destroy it, but I found none.   Ezek. 22:30

Ministering to a Prodigal

A gentle answer turns away wrath, but a harsh word stirs up anger. (Prov. 15:1)

Do to others as you would have them do to you. (Luke 6:31)

Be completely humble and gentle; be patient, bearing with one another in love. (Ephesians 4:2)

Above all, love each other deeply, because love covers over a multitude of sins. (1 Peter 4:8)

Rejoice with them that do rejoice, and weep with them that weep. (Rom. 12:15 KJV)

Finally, be ye all of one mind, having compassion one of another, love as brethren, be pitiful, be courteous. (1 Peter 3:8 KJV)

Bear ye one another's burdens, and so fulfill the law of Christ. (Gal. 6:2 KJV)

To the weak I became weak, to win the weak. I have become all things to all men so that by all possible means I might save some. (1 Corinthians 9:22)

"Ah, Sovereign LORD, you have made the heavens and the earth by your great power and outstretched arm. Nothing is too hard for you." (Jeremiah 32:17)

Thou shalt hide them in the secret of thy presence from the pride of man: thou shalt keep them secretly in a pavilion from the strife of tongues. (Ps. 31:20 KJV)

Anointing

*S*amson believed he could live any way he chose and still retain the anointing of strength on His life. When he neglected his relationship with the Lord, God allowed the power that was on him to leave him. (Judges 16) We can do nothing apart from Christ. (John 15:5)

Do not be as Samson. He took God's anointing and strength for battle for granted. He presumed that God would bless him regardless of his sin. Presumption is a dangerous thing. You must come to God often throughout the day to replenish the anointing of the Holy Spirit and then you must guard it. Receive from God moment by moment. Abide in Him and your cup will remain full. It is not about getting filled and then going your own way, trusting God to bless "Your Works." It is about His presence flowing through you as you join Him in His work.

Let us then approach the throne of grace with confidence, so that we may receive mercy and find grace to help us in our time of need. (Heb. 4:16)

I will not stagger at the promise of God through unbelief; I am strong in faith, giving glory to God; And being fully persuaded that, what he has promised, he is able also to perform. (Rom. 4:20-21 KJV)

Confess the following scriptures:

I shall decree a thing and it shall be established unto me. (Job 22:28 NAS)

I have an anointing from the Holy One and I know all things. (1 Jn. 2:20)

Rivers of living water flow from my inner being. (Jn. 4:14; Jn. 7:38)

I am the temple of God and the Spirit of God dwells in me. (1 Cor. 3:16)

I am baptized with the Holy Ghost and with fire. (Matt. 3:11; Mark 1:8; Luke 3:16; Jn. 1:33)

Greater is He that is in me than he that is in the world. (1 Jn. 4:4 NAS)

God always leads me in triumph in Christ and manifests through me the sweet aroma of the knowledge of Him in every place. (2 Cor. 2:14 NAS)

I am a servant of the Lord. He will pour out His Spirit on Me. I will prophesy (telling forth the divine counsels and predicting future events) pertaining especially to God's kingdom. (Acts 2:18 AMP)

The gifts of the Spirit operate through me. The word of wisdom, the word of knowledge, gift of faith, gift of healing, working of miracles, prophesy, discerning of spirits, tongues and interpretation. (1 Cor. 12:8-10)

Christ is the head and all things are under our feet because we are His body. I am the fullness of Christ, I am full of His power, full of miracles, full of faith, full of His word, full of His promises, full of His ability, full of His strength, full of His righteousness, full of His life. I am raised up with Christ and seated in heavenly places. (Ep. 2:6; Ep. 1:19-22)

The sovereign Lord has given me an instructed tongue to know the word that sustains the weary. (Is. 50:4)

The Spirit of the Sovereign LORD is on me, because the LORD has anointed me to preach good news to the poor. He has sent me to bind up the brokenhearted, to proclaim freedom for the captives and release from darkness for the prisoners, to proclaim the year of the LORD's favor and the day of vengeance of our God, to comfort all who mourn, and provide for those who grieve in Zion – to bestow on them a crown of beauty instead of ashes, the oil of gladness instead of mourning, and a garment of praise instead of a spirit of despair. They will be called oaks of righteousness, a planting of the LORD for the display of his splendor. (Isa. 61:1-3)

Bearing Fruit

I bear much fruit and prove to be His disciple. (Jn. 15:8 NAS)

I am a partaker of the Divine nature. (2 Peter 1:4 NAS)

I am crowned with loving kindness and compassion for others. (Ps. 103:4 NAS)

I walk and live habitually in the Holy Spirit, responsive to, controlled and guided by, His Spirit. I will not carry out the deeds of my flesh. (Gal. 5:16 AMP)

I am a servant of the New Covenant, not of the letter, but of the Spirit for the letter kills but the Spirit gives life. (2 Cor. 3:6 NAS)

I have the mind of Christ and I hold the very thoughts, purposes and intents of His heart. (1Cor. 2:16 AMP)

And let the beauty and delightfulness and favor of the Lord our God be upon us; confirm and establish the work of our hands – yes, the work of our hands, confirm and establish it. (Ps. 90:17 AMP)

And all your [spiritual] children shall be disciples [taught by the Lord and obedient to His will], and great shall be the peace and undisturbed composure of your children. You shall establish yourself in righteousness (rightness, in conformity with God's will and order): you shall be far from even the thought of oppression or destruction, for you shall not fear, and from terror, for it shall not come near you. Behold, they may gather together and stir up strife, but it is not from Me. Whoever stirs up strife against you shall fall and surrender to you. Behold, I have created the smith who blows on the fire of coals and who produces a weapon for its purpose; and I have created the devastator to destroy. But no weapon that is formed against you shall prosper, and every tongue that shall rise against you in judgment you shall show to be in the wrong. This [peace, righteousness, security, triumph over opposition] is the heritage of the servants of the Lord [those in whom the ideal Servant of the Lord is reproduced]; this is the righteousness or the vindication which they obtain from Me [this is that which I impart to them as their justification], says the Lord. (Isa. 54:13-17 AMP)

Discouragement

I will not be afraid or discouraged because of this vast army. For the battle is not mine, but God's. (2 Chron. 20:15)

Wait on the LORD; be of good courage, and He shall strengthen your heart; wait, I say, on the LORD! (Psalm 27:14 NKJ)

But the salvation of the righteous is from the LORD; He is their strength in the time of trouble. (Psalm 37:39 NKJ)

The LORD is my strength and my shield; my heart trusted in Him, and I am helped; Therefore my heart greatly rejoices, and with my song I will praise Him. (Psalm 28:7 NKJ)

Prophets of old knew that God was a just God and that He would have to judge sin. That is why they fasted, prayed and wept before God, for mercy.

..."O Lord God," I cried out; "O great and awesome God who keeps his promises and is so loving and kind to those who love and obey him! Hear my prayer! Listen carefully to what I say! Look down and see me praying night and day for your people

Israel. I confess that we have sinned against you; yes, I and my people have committed the horrible sin of not obeying the commandments you gave us through your servant Moses. Oh, please remember what you told Moses! You said, 'If you sin, I will scatter you among the nations; but if you return to me and obey my laws, even though you are exiled to the farthest corners of the earth, I will bring you back to Jerusalem. For Jerusalem is the place in which I have chosen to live.' We are your servants, the people you rescued by your great power. O Lord, please hear my prayer! Heed the prayers of those of us who delight to honor you. Please help me now as I go in and ask the king for a great favor – put it into his heart to be kind to me." (I was the king's cupbearer.) (Neh. 1:5-11 TLB)

My brothers, if one of you should wander from the truth and someone should bring him back, remember this: Whoever turns a sinner from the error of his way will save him from death and cover over a multitude of sins. (James 5:19, 20)

Power in prayer

Whatever I ask, I receive from Him because I keep His commandments and do those things that are pleasing in His sight. (1 Jn. 3:22) Because I abide in Him and His word abides in me, I ask whatever I will and it will be given unto me. (Jn. 15:7) Because I believe in Jesus I will do the same works that He did and even greater works. Whatever I ask in His name He will do that the Father may be glorified. (Jn. 14:12-14)

This is the confidence we have in approaching God: that if we ask anything according to His will, He hears us. And if we know that He hears us – whatever we ask – we know that we have what we asked of Him. (1 John 5:14-15)

I call upon you Lord, You will show me great and mighty things which I do not know. (Jer. 33:3) I lay my hands on the sick and they shall recover (Mark 16:18). The Lord will confirm the work of my hands. (Ps. 90:17 NAS) You will deliver the one who is not innocent. And he will be delivered through the cleanness of my hands. (Job 22:30) I decree a thing and it shall be established to me. (Job 22:28 NAS)

Lord, grant your servant, me your bond servant, full freedom to declare Your message fearlessly. While you stretch out Your hand to cure and perform signs and wonders through the authority and by the power of the name of Your holy child and servant Jesus. (Acts 4:29-30 AMP)

I live by faith in the Son of God. (Gal. 2:20)

The love of God is shed abroad in my heart and my faith works by this love. (Rom. 5:5; Gal. 5:6 KJV)

I overcome the enemy with the blood of the Lamb and the word of my testimony. (Rev. 12:11)

Lord let it be done unto me according to Thy word. (Luke 1:38)

I will cease striving and know that You are God. (Ps. 46:10)

Ask and it will be given to you; seek and you will find; knock and the door will be opened to you. For everyone who asks receives; he who seeks finds; and to him who knocks, the door will be opened. (Matt. 7:7-8)

He replied, "I saw Satan fall like lightning from heaven. I have given you authority to trample on snakes and scorpions and to overcome all the power of the enemy; nothing will harm you. However, do not rejoice that the spirits submit to you, but rejoice that your names are written in heaven." (Luke 10:18-20)

And I will do whatever you ask in my name, so that the Son may bring glory to the Father. You may ask me for anything in my name, and I will do it. (John 14:13-14)

If you remain in me and my words remain in you, ask whatever you wish, and it will be given you. This is to my Father's glory, that you bear much fruit, showing yourselves to be my disciples. (John 15:7-8)

In that day you will no longer ask me anything. I tell you the truth, my Father will give you whatever you ask in my name. Until now you have not asked for anything in my name. Ask and you will receive, and your joy will be complete. (John 16:23-24)

Behold! I have given you authority and power to trample upon serpents and scorpions, and [physical and mental strength and ability] over all the power that the enemy [possesses]; and nothing shall in any way harm you. (Luke 10:19 AMP)

Preaching

The Sovereign LORD has given me an instructed tongue, to know the word that sustains the weary. He wakens me morning by morning, wakens my ear to listen like one being taught. The Sovereign LORD has opened my ears, and I have not been rebellious; I have not drawn back. (Isa. 50:4-5)

The word is near me, in my mouth and in my heart. It is the word of faith that I preach. (Romans 10:8) My preaching is not persuasive words of wisdom but in demonstration of the Spirit and of power so that your faith would not rest on wisdom of men, but on the power of God. (1 Cor. 2:4-5) His word is in my heart like a fire, a fire shut up in my bones. I am weary of holding it in indeed, I cannot. (Jer. 20:9)

I will not worry beforehand or premeditate what I will speak but whatever is given me, in that hour, I will speak that for it is not I who speaks, but the Holy Spirit. (Mk. 13:11 NKJ) I am anointed to preach the gospel to the poor, He has sent me to heal the broken hearted, to preach deliverance to the captives and recovering of sight to the blind, to set at liberty them that are bruised. Because the Spirit of God is upon me and lives in me. (Luke 4:18 KJV)

Prodigal (Plans)

God's Plan vs. Enemies Plans for Your Prodigal

The thief comes only to steal and kill and destroy; I have come that they may have life, and have it to the full. (John 10:10)

Therefore Lord, "do not grant the wicked their desires, O LORD; do not let their plans succeed, or they will become proud." (Ps. 140:8)

The enemy has plans for your prodigals. But as you pray, God goes before you and He will frustrate the enemy's plans for He has already won the victory at Calvary!

_____ is the redeemed of the LORD and I say so – she/he has been redeemed from the hand of the enemy. (Ps. 107:2 KJV)

Jesus..."spoiled principalities and powers, he made a shew of them openly, triumphing over them in it." (Colossians 2:15 KJV)

"Spoiled" in the Greek, means to "totally strip of power and to undress." Jesus stripped wicked principalities and powers of their authority, jurisdiction, liberty, power, right, and strength to work in the Christian's life.

God's Plans for Your Prodigal

There is no wisdom, no insight, no plan that can succeed against the LORD. The horse is made ready for the day of battle, but victory rests with the LORD. (Prov. 21:30-31)

The Egyptians will lose heart, and I will bring their plans to nothing ... (Isa. 19:3)

When our enemies heard that we were aware of their plot and that God had frustrated it, we all returned to the wall, each to his own work. (Neh. 4:15)

Devise your strategy, but it will be thwarted; propose your plan, but it will not stand, for God is with us. (Isa. 8:10)

The LORD Almighty has sworn, "Surely, as I have planned, so it will be, and as I have purposed, so it will stand." (Isa. 14:24)

For I know the thoughts that I think toward _____, says the LORD, thoughts of peace and not of evil, to give him/her a future and a hope. Then she/he will call upon Me and go and pray to Me, and I will listen to him/her. And she/he will seek Me and find Me, when she/he searches for Me with all his/her heart. I will be found by_____, says the LORD, and I will bring her/him back from her/his captivity. (Jeremiah 29:11-14)

Your Prodigals' Plans for their lives

Many are the plans in _____'s mind, but it is Your purpose that will stand for them. (Prov. 19:21 AMP)

Trust

In you I trust, O my God. Do not let me be put to shame, nor let my enemies triumph over me. No one whose hope is in you will ever be put to shame, but they will be put to shame who are treacherous without excuse. (Ps. 25:2-3)

Some trust in chariots and some in horses, but we trust in the name of the LORD our God. They are brought to their knees and fall, but we rise up and stand firm. O LORD, save the king! Answer us when we call! (Ps. 20:7-9)

Trust in the LORD and do good; dwell in the land and enjoy safe pasture. Delight yourself in the LORD and he will give you the desires of your heart. (Ps. 37:3-4) Let Your mercy and loving-kindness come also to me, O Lord, even Your salvation according to Your promise; Then shall I have an answer for those who taunt and reproach me, for I lean on, rely on, and trust in Your word. (Ps. 119:41-42 AMP)

He will have no fear of bad news; his heart is steadfast, trusting in the LORD. His heart is secure, he will have no fear; in the end he will look in triumph on his foes. (Ps. 112:7-8)

He shall not be afraid of evil tidings; his heart is firmly fixed, trusting (leaning on and being confident) in the Lord. His heart is established and steady, he will not be afraid while he waits to see his desire established upon his adversaries. (Ps. 112:7-8 AMP)

Salvation Prayer

*G*od loves you and desires an intimate relationship with you. In fact, He loves you so much that He's not willing for you to perish or to be separated from Him. He made a way for you to live an abundant, peaceful life here on earth, and later with Him in Heaven. But sin separates us from God, and because God is also a just God, our sin must be punished.

> For the wages of sin is death, but the free gift of God is eternal life in Christ Jesus our Lord.
> Romans 6:23 (NASB)

Even though we deserve the punishment of death and separation from Him, here's the good news! God made a way to bring us close to Him. His Son, Jesus Christ, willingly gave His life to take the punishment for our sin even though we deserved it instead of Him. He took the weight of the world's sin (yours and mine) upon Himself when He willingly gave up His life to die on the cross. He took the penalty of sin, which is death, and gave His life in exchange for ours. This is called salvation.

> But God demonstrates His own love toward us, in that while we were yet sinners, Christ died for us.
> Romans 5:8 (NASB)

After Jesus died, He was buried in a tomb. On the third day He arose from the dead and was brought back to life by the power of God. He was seen by more than 500 people in 40 days before He ascended into heaven. (1 Corinthians 15:3-6)

Jesus is now seated at the right hand of God far above all rule and authority and power and dominion, and every name that is named. (Ephesians 1:20-21) He desires a personal, intimate relationship with you, and offers you the free gift of salvation. There is nothing you can do to earn this free gift. All of your good deeds could never be enough to earn it. It requires a sinless life and none of us are without sin. Only Jesus lived a sinless life. He alone was worthy to take the punishment for OUR sins. He became the payment that God required. Because of Jesus, this gift is freely given and offered to you, but now you must receive it. Now **ALL** of your sins can be forgiven not because you are so good, but because of what Jesus has done for you.

For by grace you have been saved through faith; and that not of yourselves, it is the gift of God; not as a result of works, that no one should boast.

Ephesians 2:8-9 (NASB)

Do you believe that Jesus is the Son of God and that He was raised from the dead? Will you turn from your sin in repentance? Will you embrace the sacrifice of Jesus as payment for your sin? Will you receive Jesus as your Lord and Savior? Will you receive the gift of eternal life?

God is offering the gift of salvation to you, but in order to receive it you must ...

☐ Believe that Jesus Christ is Lord – the Son of God, and that God raised Him from the dead.
   And there is salvation in no one else; for there is no other name under heaven that has been given among men, by which we must be saved. Acts 4:12 (NASB)

☐ Admit that you have sinned.
   For all have sinned and fall short of the glory of God.   Romans 3:23

☐ Confess those sins to God, asking Him to forgive you of every one of them, even the ones you don't remember. His forgiveness has been offered to you whether you have sinned a little or sinned a lot.
   If we confess our sins, He is faithful and righteous to forgive us our sins and to cleanse us from all unrighteousness.   1 John 1:9 (NASB)

☐ Receive Jesus Christ as your Lord and Savior.
   But as many as received Him, to them He gave the right to become children of God, even to those who believe in His name.   John 1:129 NASB)

If you would like to receive the free gift of salvation, then pray this prayer with me now:

Father, I believe that Jesus is Your Son, and that He died for my sin on the cross and rose from the dead. Forgive me for my sin. I am sorry for going my own way; now I want to go Your way. Come into my heart, Lord Jesus. I surrender my life to You. Amen.

If you believe this in your heart and sincerely prayed this prayer, you have become a child of God. You now have a new Lord and Savior, One who loves you very much — Jesus Christ. In Him you are a new creation. (2 Cor. 5:17-18) All your past sins and mistakes are forgiven, no matter how bad they were. A baby is a new creation. Does it have a past? No, of course not, and now neither do you. The slate has been wiped clean.

Resources

And [God] Who provides seed for the sower and bread for
eating will also provide and multiply your [resources for] sowing
and increase the fruits of your righteousness …
2 Corinthians 9:10 (AMP)

Expect the Harvest!

The following pages are resources we offer to help make your prayer warrior and intercessor journey easier and more productive for you and your loved ones. Use them with the expectation that the Holy Spirit will work in you and through you to touch the hearts of your loved ones. And by all means, be blessed – He longs to shower you with His blessings, dear one.

Prodigal Prayer Meeting

Walking in the Land of the Heart

*W*hen Joshua and the Israelites went in to take their promised land, the Lord instructed them to help each other possess their land before they could enjoy their own Promised Land.

> [13]The LORD your God is giving you rest and has granted you this land. [14]Your wives, your children and your livestock may stay in the land that Moses gave you east of the Jordan, but all your fighting men, fully armed, must cross over ahead of your brothers. You are to help your brothers [15]until the LORD gives them rest, as he has done for you, and until they too have taken possession of the land that the LORD your God is giving them. After that, you may go back and occupy your own land, which Moses the servant of the LORD gave you east of the Jordan toward the sunrise.
>
> Joshua 1:13-15

Today, in the spiritual realm, we call this corporate prayer. When things get tough, find a prayer partner to stand with you! Or, even better, start a prodigal prayer group!

Leader's Guide

Recommended time segments provide for 1½ hour sessions. An ideal class size is 10-13 members. Although fewer is acceptable, it is highly recommended that you allow no more than 15 in order to encourage intimacy within the group.

Materials Needed:

Leader: "Mud on My Knees" Manual; Praying Prodigals Home Audio and Bible. You will find instruction to teach others how to set up their journal at the beginning of this manual.

Students: Bible, Journal and Praying Prodigal's Home CD and printed, "Mud on My Knees" manual.

Leader Check List:

☐ As a leader, you are the example of what God will do when you spend time with Him, so you must be sure that you pray and journal daily.
☐ Prepare for the group: Pray for your group and know the material. This will also help you understand the thought processes that others go through. Be sensitive to the Holy Spirit.
☐ It is vital for you to keep your heart right with God so that you can hear Him clearly.
☐ Follow the Holy Spirit's leadership, and do not be afraid of silence. This is when God may be speaking to someone's heart.

Three Types of Leaders:

1. The first leader is concerned about what others will think about her or about the mistakes she may make in leading.
2. The second type of leader is concerned about getting all of the material finished in the allotted time.
3. The third leader is concerned about what God is doing in the hearts of those present.

It is the third leader that will have the most success in helping others become more intimate with God. When you are sensitive to the Holy Spirit, you can lead your group into this relationship. If you sense that God is doing a work in someone's heart, stop and ask if anyone would like to share what's on her/his heart.

☐ You set the tone for the group, so to put the others at ease, take the lead and the group will follow your example.

☐ Allow each person an opportunity to share and pray so no one individual dominates the conversation or prayer.
☐ The leader's role is essential in:
  1. Establishing a warm and friendly atmosphere of acceptance
  2. Welcoming each person
  3. Encouraging participation
  4. Praying for each person
  5. Leading others in prayer
  6. Managing the group
☐ Open each session in prayer.
☐ Confidentiality is a very important key factor. Explain that what is shared in the group must stay in the group and not be shared with others, including spouses.
☐ Allow time for questions at the end of each session.

Opening Ice Breaker: Ask each person to introduce themselves and complete the following sentence: "One thing no one here knows about me is ..."

Introductory Meeting

Leading:
- Open with prayer
- Write down the first name of each prodigal that your group will be praying for.
- Read the introduction pages of Mud on Your Knees workbook together. Stress the importance of committing to at least 45 minutes a day in study, prayer and journaling.
- Listen to the audio, Praying Your Prodigals Home CD together (20-25 minutes). Instruct each person to use this CD during their personal prayer time.
- Encourage group members to be sensitive to the Holy Spirit and to make a note of anything God brings to their mind. He may be trying to get their attention. The note will serve as a reminder to journal or pray about it later.

Question and Answer Time:
- Group members might ask questions that you do not know the answer to. Encourage them to search the scriptures before they come to the next meeting.
- Allow time for members to share testimonies of what God is doing.

Teaching:
- Remind members to pray daily for the list of prodigals represented within the group.

- Instruct them to do daily lessons in their workbook and stress the importance of praying and journaling each day.
- Use the meeting format outlined on the following pages, or you can stretch it out over a longer period using one lesson per week or one per month.
- Encourage each person to pray along with the Praying Your Prodigals Home CD. This will teach them how to pray scripture.

Be Sensitive to God:
- If God interrupts your agenda, wait on Him and allow Him time to move. Be sensitive to the leading of the Holy Spirit.
- Close in prayer.

Suggested Schedule

Introductory Meeting

A Personal Word from the Author

How to Guide

Personal Prayer Garden

Their Hearts, Your Garden

Gardening in the Old and New Testament

Week 1

Week 1 – Day 1: Gardening in the Hearts of Man

Week 1 – Day 2: Aim for the Heart

Week 1 – Day 3: Soil Preparation

Week 1 – Day 4: Digging Up Rocks: Cultivating Your Heart

Week 1 – Day 5: A Backslidden Heart

Week 5 – Day 3: God's Power; Authority

Week 5 – Day 4: The Kingdom of God

Week 5 – Day 5: Binding and Loosing; The Blood of Jesus

Week 6

Week 6 – Day 1: Empowered with the Holy Spirit

Week 6 – Day 2: The Gardeners Protection

Week 6 – Day 3: Abiding in the Vine; Connected to the Vine

Week 6 – Day 4: Pruning; Washing with the Word

Week 6 – Day 5: Letting Go and Letting God; Time; Landscaping; Harvest; A Word of Caution; A Final Word

Every Week:

- Open in prayer
- Start and end the meeting on time
- Review the material, ask:
- What truth, concept or scripture, stood out to you this week? (Be prepared to discuss the material).
- Did the Lord show you anything?
- Did you struggle with anything?
- Have a "formal" Question and Answer Period
- Share specific prayer requests
- Use the remaining time for corporate prayer
- Depending on the size of your group, you can pray as a group or break off into smaller groups.
- Keep a Group Journal of answered prayer

We would love to hear your testimonies about what God has done through your group. You can email them to: info@gardenoftheheart.com.

Prayer Journal Forms

*T*he following pages contain forms you can use to build your own personal prayer garden, tools to help you prepare, sow, cultivate and harvest the garden of your family's hearts. OK warriors, time for battle!

There is no right or wrong way to use the forms throughout this resource. Be creative and use this journal whichever way works best for you. For example, I use the *Sowing & Reaping* forms to pray for my husband, children, myself and my prodigals. I use the *Pray & Write* forms throughout this resource to create prayer lists such as Ministries, Extended Family, Friend's Requests, etc. Or I place a name and request next to a scripture promise in the Seed Section with a date.

Create a <u>Personalized Prayer Schedule</u> that works for you. My <u>Prayer Schedule</u> looks like this. Daily, I pray different categories of scriptures for my family, such as those found on pages 163–166 (heart scriptures, strongholds, weed killer scriptures) and add other categories. This covers my loved ones who are prodigals and those with hearts starting to grow cold. And this allows me to pray proactively to protect all of our hearts from drifting away from God. I then focus on one family member each day. And add the other prayer lists I have created to different days of the week. For example, on Mondays I pray for all *Prodigals*. On Saturdays, I pray specifically for *Friend's Requests* and Sundays are designated for *Ministries*.

I use the *Journaling* pages for prayer directives from God or a place to work out a struggle I may encounter while praying. I use the *Notes* pages throughout this manual to add other teaching and revelation about intercessory prayer. This allows me to keep everything that I am learning at my fingerprints.

SOWING SEEDS

*A*dd a picture to the first page of someone you are praying for. Give it a try.

This will help you to connect with those for whom you are praying. There is something about seeing their face when you pray. You will be reminded of your love for them and God's plans for their lives.

Additional Scriptures

Add other scriptures that speak to you in this section. Be sure to include reference address and Scripture version that spoke most to you.

Additional Scriptures

Add other scriptures that speak to you in this section. Be sure to include

reference address and Scripture version that spoke most to you.

Additional Scriptures

*A*dd other scriptures that speak to you in this section. Be sure to include

reference address and Scripture version that spoke most to you.

Additional Scriptures

*A*dd other scriptures that speak to you in this section. Be sure to include reference address and Scripture version that spoke most to you.

Journaling Pages

Date

Journaling Pages

Date

Journaling Pages

Date

Journaling Pages

Date

Journaling Pages

Date

Journaling Pages

Date

Journaling Pages

Date

Journaling Pages

Date

Pray & Write . . .

Sowing & Reaping

$\mathcal{U}$se these forms to keep track of God's faithfulness. Write the specific prayer request you've prayed for your loved one; now, add a scripture for the promises you've claimed on their behalf. Date your entry and watch to see what God will do (we wrote in a sample to help you get started)! Be sure to record His answers – reap the harvest you helped God create!

Prayer Journal

Praying for: _____ *Tommy* _____ (sample) _____

Date	Sowing	Date	Reaping - Harvest
6-1-13	Father, remove the veil from his heart	7-15-08	He called & asked for prayer
	Soft heart, praying heart Scriptures, p. 163-165		
7-7-13	Restoration w/father	9-15-08	Had lunch with father
	Mal. 4:6		
8-10-13	Bad friends, drinking		
	2 Cor. 6:17		

Prayer Journal

Praying for: _____

Date	Sowing	Date	Reaping - Harvest

Prayer Journal

Praying for: _____

Date	Sowing	Date	Reaping - Harvest

Prayer Journal

Praying for: _____

Date	Sowing	Date	Reaping - Harvest

Prayer Journal

Praying for: _____

Date	Sowing	Date	Reaping - Harvest

Prayer Journal

Praying for: _____

Date	Sowing	Date	Reaping - Harvest

Prayer Journal

Praying for: _____

Date	Sowing	Date	Reaping - Harvest

Prayer Journal

Praying for: _____

Date	Sowing	Date	Reaping - Harvest

Prayer Journal

Praying for: _____

Date	Sowing	Date	Reaping - Harvest

Prayer Journal

Praying for: _____

Date	Sowing	Date	Reaping - Harvest

Notes. . .

About the Author

$\mathcal{D}$ebra Bosacki is Director of Garden of the Heart Ministries. She resides with her husband, Geno, in Wisconsin. They have five grown children.

Debra is a life coach, author, speaker and writer. She co-authored "Washing With the Word Journal."

Garden of the Heart Ministries is a non-denominational ministry whose purpose is to draw Christians into greater intimacy with God and equip them with tools to grow strong in the Lord. Within our web site, www.gardenoftheheart.com, you will find teaching on Spiritual Journaling, Prayer, Healing, and other topics related to your walk with God.

A WORD FROM THE AUTHOR:

My greatest gratitude goes to my Lord and Savior Who inspired this work and Who ...makes the garden grow in our hearts. (1 Corinthians 3:6 TLB)

A special thanks to my wonderful husband Geno, for his love, patience and encouragement; and to my children, Corissa, Joel, Jacob, Jeanna, and Katie; and my sister, Cindy O'Leary, for their love and support.

I wish to acknowledge and thank Kathy Boncher – retired, co-founder of Garden of the Heart Ministries, for her prayer support, investment of time and contribution to this work. Thank you Kathy for your faithfulness in coming alongside of me and supporting the vision that God birthed in my heart.

Many thanks and great appreciation goes to my editor, Mary Deckert for her time, advice, ideas, input, editing expertise and devotion to this project! Thank you for seeing it through to completion and helping me fulfill the ministry that God has called me to.

And a special thanks to my close friends for their suggestions, encouragement and prayer support.

One plants, one waters, but it is God who gives the increase!

I pray your eyes will be opened to the magnitude of the truth within this resource and that you will be motivated to pray more fervently.

I am brought once again to my knees in gratitude, with Psalm 138:1 on my heart as I close this book and leave you to cultivate God's garden in the hearts of your loved ones. May it minister to you as you co-labor with Christ and sink your own knees mud deep in the soil of your loved one's hearts!

> [A David Psalm] Thank you! Everything in me says "Thank you!" Angels listen as I sing my thanks. I kneel in worship facing your holy temple and say it again: "Thank you!" Thank you for your love, thank you for your faithfulness; Most holy is your name, most holy is your Word. The moment I called out, you stepped in; you made my life large with strength.   Psalm 138:1-3 (MSG)

His Richest Blessings,

Debra Bosacki

Made in the USA
Middletown, DE
16 March 2018